THE LORD IS MY

SHEPHERD

THE TWENTY-THIRD PSALM

CLARENCE SEXTON

THE LORD IS MY SHEPHERD

SECOND EDITION
COPYRIGHT
DECEMBER 2004

CROWN
CHRISTIAN
PUBLICATIONS
Royal Reading

1700 BEAVER CREEK DRIVE
POWELL, TENNESSEE ◆ 37849

1-877 AT CROWN

SUNDAY SCHOOL SERIES

THE LORD IS MY SHEPHERD

Copyright © 2004

Crown Christian Publications

Powell, Tennessee 37849

ISBN: 1-58981-249-2

Layout and design by Stephen Troell

Printed in the United States of America

DEDICATION

This book is affectionately dedicated to Lucille Caughron. This wonderful Christian lady is the mother of my wife. She is the Christian whom God used in the formative part of my ministry to encourage me greatly in the Lord.

APPRECIATION

I want to express my deepest appreciation to Tim and Angie Tomlinson for their work in preparing this book for publication. May the Lord bless them in a special way for their labor.

TABLE OF CONTENTS

Sexton Family — 1954

In 1946, Preston Thomas Sexton and Ruby Lee Stanley were united in marriage. Soon after they were married, Preston bought his new bride a beautiful new family Bible. I was the first of four children born to this couple.

While growing up, I enjoyed looking through the big family Bible. The most fascinating thing in that Bible to me was the beautiful insert displaying the Twenty-third Psalm. A page from that wonderful psalm is reproduced here just as it appears in that family Bible. May God bless you as you read, memorize, and meditate on the Twenty-third Psalm.

Clarence Sexton

Acts 5:42

The Twenty Third Psalm

A PSALM OF DAVID

The Lord is my Shepherd; I shall not want.

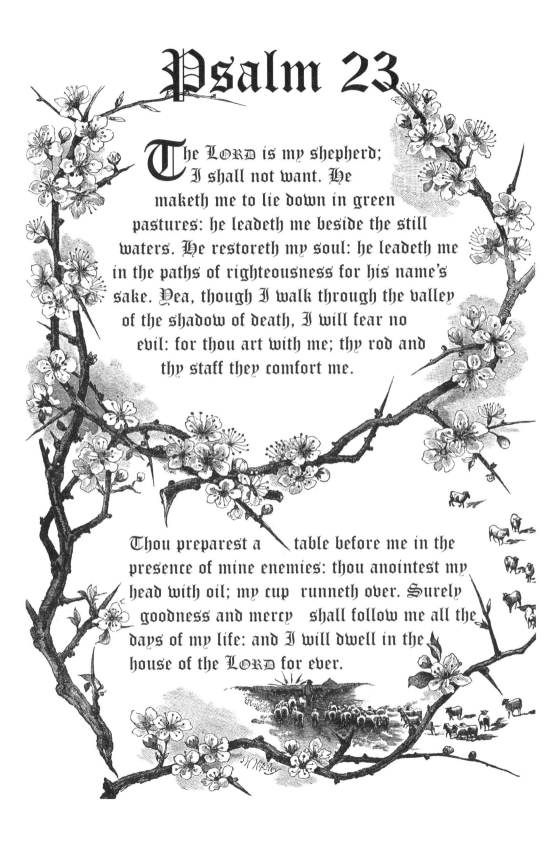

Psalm 23

The LORD is my shepherd; I shall not want. He maketh me to lie down in green pastures: he leadeth me beside the still waters. He restoreth my soul: he leadeth me in the paths of righteousness for his name's sake. Yea, though I walk through the valley of the shadow of death, I will fear no evil: for thou art with me; thy rod and thy staff they comfort me.

Thou preparest a table before me in the presence of mine enemies: thou anointest my head with oil; my cup runneth over. Surely goodness and mercy shall follow me all the days of my life: and I will dwell in the house of the LORD for ever.

God Found His Man

MEET THE MAN AFTER GOD'S OWN HEART

"And the LORD said unto Samuel, How long wilt thou mourn for Saul, seeing I have rejected him from reigning over Israel? fill thine horn with oil, and go, I will send thee to Jesse the Bethlehemite: for I have provided me a king among his sons."

I Samuel 16:1

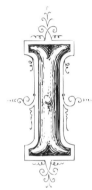 n the closing days of his life, the prophet Samuel was heavy-hearted over the condition of the kingdom, and in particular, over what he found in the life of King Saul. God had rejected Saul. Israel desperately needed leadership. Something had to be done. The man of God had a broken heart as he thought about his nation.

In I Samuel 16:1 we read,

And the LORD said unto Samuel, How long wilt thou mourn for Saul, seeing I have rejected him from reigning over Israel? fill thine horn with oil, and go, I will send thee to Jesse the Bethlehemite: for I have provided me a king among his sons.

David is mentioned 1,127 times in the Bible. The apostle Paul is mentioned 163 times in the Bible. Just a handful of chapters are given to Abraham and Joseph. However, fifty-four chapters of the Bible are given to the life of David, not including the Psalms.

Our God has placed an unmistakable emphasis on the life of David. What is there about this man that God wants us to know that is so vital that He speaks of him over a thousand times in His Word?

In I Samuel 16:1, God announced, *"I have provided me a king."* Then He instructed Samuel in verse three, *"Thou shalt anoint unto me him whom I name unto thee."*

God did a wonderful work in David's life to enable him to lead his entire generation. God said, *"I have provided me a king."*

The Lord still searches for those He can bless and use. He is searching this very moment for those who have a heart for Him. He sees what men do not see. He looks where men cannot look. He spies out our spiritual lives and sees what is in our hearts.

An often overlooked principle unfolds in this Bible scene. It is that God begins something long before men ever see evidence of it. Saul had been rejected long before the people saw it because God saw in the heart of Saul something that He *could not* bless. In the same way, David had been chosen long before the nation ever recognized him because God saw something He *could* bless in the heart of David.

God raises up people to do mighty things. He searches for those who have a heart for Him. God has already made a plan to bless in an outstanding way, a way that is far beyond what we ordinarily witness. He is still looking. Oh, how we should desire God to find what He is looking for in our lives!

The Lord searches for those who have a heart for Him.

In every town and every village, in every city and every church, in every part of the country and in every country of the world, God is still looking. God is looking in your neighborhood; God is looking in your workplace. God is looking in your school. He is looking for someone to bless and use. Do you want to be one of those people? If you do and if you desire God with all your heart, I promise you, God will find you.

15

All of us are doing as much for God as we desire to do. All of us are at the stage in our Christian lives where we desire to be. We are content to be what we are. We do not go any farther with the Lord until we have a desire to do so. God can work in our hearts to create this desire. We must be willing to pray, "Lord, bless me and use me for Your glory."

The Lord Is in Control

It looked to Samuel as if the kingdom were out of control. Saul's life was certainly out of control, but God was still in control. We seem to have the idea that when things around us are falling apart, the whole world must be coming apart at the seams as well.

When we see families torn apart or experience difficulties in our own lives or in the life of the church that we are attending, we need to be reminded that God is still in control. He has never lost the reins.

In Philippians 4:5, Paul exhorted believers, *"Let your moderation be known unto all men. The Lord is at hand."* Some people think this verse means that the Lord is always near. Others believe that this verse means the Lord's return is near. Both are true. The Lord is near and the Lord's return is near. *"The Lord is at hand."*

He continues in Philippians 4:6-7,

> *Be careful for nothing; but in every thing by prayer and supplication with thanksgiving let your requests be made known unto God. And the peace of God, which passeth all understanding, shall keep your hearts and minds through Christ Jesus.*

If we will remember that *"the Lord is at hand,"* then we can *"be careful for nothing."* Most often, when we quote this passage we quote verses six and seven together and leave out verse five. However, we are not going to be able to obey the command of verse six if we leave out verse five. For us not to worry, we must realize that *"the Lord is at hand."* When we realize this, we can *"be careful for nothing."* We need not worry about anything because God is in control.

As an old man, Samuel carried a crushing burden. His mother, Hannah, prayed before Samuel was born that God would give her a son. She promised the Lord that she would give that son back to Him. Dedicated to God before birth, his whole life had been given to serving the Lord. He even established a school of prophets to train men to serve the Lord.

However, the people had asked for a king. Samuel, as their spiritual leader, felt he had been rejected. Israel wanted to be like every other nation. God granted their request, and carnal Saul came to reign as king in Israel.

Everything the old prophet had given his life to seemed to be in vain. He was greatly troubled. In a loving rebuke, God spoke to him in the first verse of I Samuel 16, *"How long wilt thou mourn for Saul?"* In so many words, "Samuel, how long are you going to be upset about this? How long will you live without trusting Me in this matter?"

We all have people and things that are difficult to give to God. You may believe that you cannot let go of your children. However, it is not that you cannot; it is that you will not. You may not trust your loved one to do the right thing; however, you must trust God to do the right thing with that person. Final surrender to God does not necessarily mean that God is going to move in a flash to do something; but it does mean that the moment we commit it to God, He will give us peace in knowing that He *will* take care of it.

God asked Samuel, "How long will you worry and fret? How long will you think that this is your nation and your people and not My nation and My people?" Many times the Lord has said to me, "How long will you think that this is your church and these are your people?" The church is the Lord's, and these are His people. It is His work.

17

As I yield my life to God and give my children to the Lord, realizing they are a gift from Him, I find a wonderfully sweet peace. Realizing that God is in control is a blessing and a comfort to my heart.

God said in I Samuel 16:1, *"How long wilt thou mourn for Saul, seeing I have rejected him from reigning over Israel?"*

The Lord commanded Samuel to fill his horn with oil and go to Bethlehem to anoint a king. He said to Samuel, "Make the journey to Jesse's house. I have found a king. I want you to anoint him." There can be no doubt, God is in control!

The Lord Is Always Working

We may not always see God's work, but He is always working. He was preparing David when no one knew much about him except the Lord. If you read carefully the sixteenth chapter, you will see that God dealt with Samuel, then Jesse, then Jesse's sons, then finally God dealt with David. God dealt with each one in a different way.

Full of worry and fretting, Samuel had to learn that God was in control. Of his eight sons and two daughters, Jesse surely believed that God would use one of his children. And He was just as certain that David was not the one. When seven of his sons were rejected and the horn of oil was not poured on them, God had to deal with them. Many people sit in our churches who do not have the horn of oil poured on them; God must deal with them.

Finally, the Lord was at work in David's life. David was a shepherd. He had the heart of a shepherd. Later we read that he was willing to risk his life and to give his life, if necessary, for one of his sheep. God was doing something in the life of this shepherd boy, for God is always at work.

The Lord told the old prophet, "Go down to Jesse's house." Samuel said, "I can't go; Saul will kill me." God said, "You tell him that you are going to offer a sacrifice. Meet with Jesse and his family alone. Have his sons brought before you, and I will show you that I have provided Myself a king."

Jesse's sons were brought before Samuel. Seven of his sons appeared, but the eighth was still out tending the sheep. One by one they came before Samuel and God said, "That's not the one; that's not the one; that's not the one." Finally, when they had all passed, Samuel said to Jesse, "Are all of your sons here?"

Many times we believe that great things cannot be done. Recently, I read of a man conducting experiments with fish. He placed a large fish in a tank along with several minnows. The large fish consumed all the minnows. Then, he put more minnows inside the tank, but within a glass enclosure. The fish would attempt to attack them, but he could not get to them. Finally, the man released the minnows from the enclosure. But, the fish would not move. He had learned that he could not get to them, so he would no longer try. The fish had been conditioned to believe that it could not be done.

We allow our minds to be conditioned to believe that God is not going to do great things. We think, "God may work somewhere else, but He is not going to work here." But God is always working. We should desire for God to do a mighty work in our lives and in the lives of our families and churches.

The Lord Uses People
Whom Others Overlook

Samuel said to Jesse, "Are these all your boys?" He said, "I have another young son in the field keeping the sheep." Because he was able to send someone else to care for the sheep, Jesse could have already brought David in from the field had he thought that God might use him.

Knowing David and the heart he had for God, can you imagine how he would have loved to have been in that meeting with Samuel? He would have thought it the greatest privilege of his life to be there when the prophet Samuel came on his journey from Ramah. But he was overlooked and forgotten.

Many things must have gone through the mind of Samuel on his journey to Bethlehem. Now, thinking that he has seen all of Jesse's boys but one and knowing that God had said one of Jesse's sons was to be the king, can you imagine how Samuel felt as he was waiting for David to arrive? Suddenly, David arrived at the house. Face to face stood the young shepherd and the prophet. "This is My king," Samuel heard God say. Hands trembling with excitement, Samuel reached inside his garment for the oil, and David, standing there before his father and his brethren, was anointed by Samuel. The oil ran from David's body and dripped to the ground.

You see, God uses people whom others have overlooked. This is what Paul meant when he wrote,

> *For ye see your calling, brethren, how that not many wise men after the flesh, not many mighty, not many noble, are called: But God hath chosen the foolish things of the world to confound the wise; and God hath chosen the weak things of the world to confound the things which are mighty; And base things of the world, and things which are despised, hath God chosen, yea, and things which are not, to bring to nought things that are: That no flesh should glory in his presence* (I Corinthians 1:26-29).

God works in such a way that He gets the glory and men do not. If we begin to steal His glory, He will stop blessing. The glory belongs to the Lord, not to men. Praise God for salvation. Praise God for His mercy and grace. I thank God that I have been redeemed. I praise the Lord that He has forgiven my sin and that He is my Savior. Salvation is the starting point, and God desires to finish the work that He has started in all our lives.

Recently, my wife and I were in a fast-food restaurant. A lady and a young boy, just a short distance away, caught my attention. I do not think the child had any idea that I was watching him and his mother. My mind traveled back to my childhood. I could see myself standing there with my mother. I saw myself in that boy in so many ways. My mind was flooded with memories. I recognized him, and I felt that he probably recognized me because he attended our church. On the way out, the mother spoke to me and said, "Hello, Pastor Sexton." I greeted the mother and her son.

As that boy stood there with his mother, perhaps he thought, "This is my pastor. He is someone special, someone important." Maybe he started thinking about himself. However, God sees things far differently than we do. When that child passed by me, I could not help thinking, "He may be the next pastor of our church."

There is a God in heaven who desires to bless and use us. Allow Him to bless and use you as He desires.

The Glory Due His Name

An Introduction to the Psalms

"Give unto the LORD the glory due unto his name; worship the LORD in the beauty of holiness."

Psalm 29:2

---

ooking at the Psalms collectively, we find that Psalm 29:2 is the key verse for the entire book. The Bible says, *"Give unto the LORD the glory due unto his name; worship the LORD in the beauty of holiness."* This word *"glory"* has to do with what rightly belongs to the Lord.

In Psalm 148:13 the Bible says, *"Let them praise the name of the LORD: for his name alone is excellent; his glory is above the earth and heaven."*

The glory that rightly belongs to God is *"above the earth and heaven."* We cannot humanly comprehend it. If we follow what God says in Psalm 29:2, ascribing to God the glory due to Him, we shall never be able to exhaust that glory. Nor can we ever fully comprehend or express that glory.

The Bible teaches us that we should live our lives so that they bring glory to the Lord. The life of every child of God should bring glory to His name. Bringing glory to Gods name is giving to the Lord what is rightly His.

Neglecting to give God glory is the source of trouble in our world. Paul stated that the sinful condition is a result of failing to give God what rightly belongs to Him.

Because that which may be known of God is manifest in them; for God hath shewed it unto them.

*For the invisible things of him from the creation of
the world are clearly seen, being understood by the
things that are made, even his eternal power and
Godhead; so that they are without excuse: because
that, when they knew God, they glorified him not as
God, neither were thankful; but became vain in their
imaginations, and their foolish heart was darkened.
Professing themselves to be wise, they became fools*
(Romans 1:19-22).

Notice verse twenty-one, *"Because that, when they knew God,
they glorified him not as God."*

We find in the Bible that man has knowledge of God through
creation and conscience. We have enough of the knowledge of God
to condemn us but not enough of the knowledge of God to save us.
In other words, in the heavens and the earth which declare His
glory, and in the conscience, which God has put in us, we have
enough of the knowledge of God to help us realize that we are
sinners and that we need Him. We must hear the wonderful good
news of the gospel in order to be saved, but from the conscience and
creation we should begin to glorify God.

When a man turns from the knowledge that there is a God,
instead of being enlightened, his foolish heart is darkened. The
Word of God says in verse twenty-two, *"Professing themselves to
be wise, they became fools."*

In the fourth chapter of the Revelation of Jesus Christ, a scene
unfolds before us. It is the account of the judgment seat of Christ,
where we shall stand before Jesus Christ and place our crowns at
His feet, declaring that He alone is worthy.

*And when those beasts give glory and honour and
thanks to him that sat on the throne, who liveth for
ever and ever, The four and twenty elders fall down
before him that sat on the throne, and worship him*

that liveth for ever and ever, and cast their crowns before the throne, saying, Thou art worthy, O Lord, to receive glory and honour and power: for thou hast created all things, and for thy pleasure they are and were created (Revelation 4:9-11).

John records in verse eleven, *"Thou art worthy, O Lord, to receive glory and honour and power: for thou hast created all things, and for thy pleasure they are and were created."*

> *Perhaps the greatest indictment against Christians and against the church is our failure to bring the glory to the Lord that is due His name.*

The Word of God says that at the end of the way we shall declare, with the mind of Christ in a redeemed body, that God deserves all the glory. If we know this is how the end will unfold, we understand that we should give Him the glory that is due His name.

Are we glorifying God by the way we live and by what we say? Perhaps the greatest indictment against Christians and against the church is our failure to bring the glory to the Lord that is due His name. Let us look at what God's Word says about His name.

Neither is there salvation in any other: for there is none other name under heaven given among men, whereby we must be saved (Acts 4:12).

No wonder God says, *"The glory due unto His name."* There is no other name under heaven whereby we must be saved.

> *Wherefore God also hath highly exalted him, and given him a name which is above every name: that at the name of Jesus every knee should bow, of things in heaven, and things in earth, and things under the earth; and that every tongue should confess that Jesus Christ is Lord, to the glory of God the Father* (Philippians 2:9-11).

One vital thing must be found in our churches. There may be friendliness, warm-hearted people, preaching, and singing, but the Bible says in Ephesians 3:21, *"Unto him be glory in the church by Christ Jesus throughout all ages, world without end. Amen."*

We must find glory in the church, the glory that is due His name. We have glory in the church when we pay the tithe, when we pray, and when we sing from the overflow of a Spirit-filled life. We have glory in the church when we preach and when Jesus Christ can be seen in the preaching. We find glory in the church in the spirit of our worship when we come to honor and adore our Lord. When we leave we should be able to say, "There was glory given to God in that place. There was glory in the church."

Give God Glory for His Person

Notice the word *"give"* in Psalm 29:2. We are to *give* unto the Lord. The word *"give"* means "to ascribe honor." The Word of God says in Psalm 29:1-2, *"Give unto the LORD, O ye mighty, give unto the LORD glory and strength. Give unto the LORD the glory due unto his name; worship the LORD in the beauty of holiness."*

When the Hebrew people became polytheistic, worshipers of many gods, God had them carried away into Babylonian exile. Among the Babylonians, who worshiped many gods, the Jews had burned into their hearts this fact, "The Lord, He is one God." After they came out of exile, they remained a monotheistic people declaring that there is no god in all the earth but their God.

27

We believe that God is real; we believe in God the Father, God the Son, and God the Holy Spirit. We believe that God the Holy Spirit is co-equal and co-existent with God the Father and God the Son. We believe that God the Son is co-equal, co-existent, eternally existent with God the Father and God the Holy Spirit. We believe in the Trinity. We believe that there is no god like our God.

When Moses stood before the Pharaoh and the gods of Egypt challenged the God of the Hebrews, the Egyptians finally said to Pharaoh, "This thing that is happening is the finger of God. Our gods are not like their God."

We are living in a land that has become pantheistic–god is all and all is god. We are living in a garden of gods where men are being taught that they are gods. God's people need to live so that their lives give glory to God. The world around us needs to know that there is no god like our God. We should give Him glory for His person, glory for who He is.

The Creator who spoke this universe into existence lives within each believer. We are the temple of God. No other god is like our God. He made the sun, moon, and stars. He opened up the Red Sea and brought the newborn nation of Israel through on dry ground. No other god can do these mighty miracles. The Lord says, "Give Me glory because of who I am."

The Lord Jesus is due glory for His person. I know God personally. I give Him glory for His person–not for what He has done, but for who He is. In Isaiah 44:6 the prophet cries, *"Thus saith the LORD the King of Israel, and his redeemer the LORD of hosts; I am the first, and I am the last; and beside me there is no God."*

Verse eight says, *"Fear ye not, neither be afraid: have not I told thee from that time, and have declared it? ye are even my witnesses. Is there a God beside me? yea, there is no God; I know not any."*

Because someone told us of Christ and we were born again, we know the only true and living God as our personal Savior. He deserves glory for His person.

Give God Glory for His Power

We should give Him glory for His power. In Psalm 29:3 we read, *"The voice of the LORD is upon the waters."*

Here under the inspiration of the Holy Spirit, David paints a powerful word picture of a storm. If you are familiar with the geography and the topography of the land of the Bible, you can imagine the storm starting out in the Mediterranean Sea and moving to the land. The word *"Sirion"* was used. This is a Sidonian term for Mount Hermon. David described a storm sweeping across the Mediterranean Sea touching the north of the Bible lands. It shook all the land. It moved to the far south in Kadesh and even shook the foundation stones of Petra, the city carved out of stone. The psalmist stood in awe as he considered this storm. He saw the power of God in it and said, "When I see God's power, I know there is glory due to the Lord for His power."

> *The voice of the LORD is upon the waters: the God of glory thundereth: the LORD is upon many waters. The voice of the LORD is powerful; the voice of the LORD is full of majesty. The voice of the LORD breaketh the cedars; yea, the LORD breaketh the cedars of Lebanon* (Psalm 29:3-5).

This thundering from heaven is identified as the voice of God. David said, "As the storm moves and the thunder sounds, we recognize the voice of God. The voice of God comes across the waters as He rides the sea. The Almighty comes across the waters to land and shakes the land. God strikes the mighty cedars of Lebanon."

David continued in verse six, *"He maketh them also to skip like a calf; Lebanon and Sirion like a young unicorn."* He was speaking here of mountains. God said that He makes the mountains skip, move, and quiver like a wild beast. This is the power of God. Verse seven says, *"The voice of the LORD divideth the flames of fire."* This describes the flash of lightning breaking from the sky. As the raging of the heavens meets the raging of the sea, the psalmist says, "I see in all this the majesty and power of God. Glory is due unto our God who can do this."

The description continues in verses eight and nine, *"The voice of the LORD shaketh the wilderness; the LORD shaketh the wilderness of Kadesh. The voice of the LORD maketh the hinds to calve...."* We are told in the book of Job that the hind had a difficult time delivering her young. Here God says that the voice of God is so mighty that the hinds quiver with fear and deliver their young prematurely. *"...and discovereth the forests..."* The secret, dark places in the woods that no one knows are revealed by the storm. *"...and in his temple doth every one speak of his glory."*

> *Our Lord not only gives us peace but peace in the storm.*

The storm started out at sea and then moved to the land. As it struck the land, some of the mighty cedars of Lebanon were torn by the voice of God. He moved from the cedars to the mountains making the very mountains quake. He flung the storm down from the north across the land to the south. He roared into the wilderness shaking it

30

and the rock foundations of Petra. The Bible says that as this storm raged all around, the people sat inside the temple of God and declared, "The Lord is due glory. Listen to His voice. Watch the lightning flash. Feel the earth quiver. He is due glory for His power."

Give God Glory for His Peace

The faithless person does not understand our God who can sweep across the sea, break across the shore, rip down the mighty cedars of Lebanon, shake the mountains, rage across the wilderness and move the foundations of the city and yet be so personal that He can give us peace in our hearts. Our Lord not only gives us peace but peace in the storm. We should give Him glory for His peace.

> *The LORD sitteth upon the flood; yea, the LORD sitteth King for ever. The LORD will give strength unto his people; the LORD will bless his people with peace* (Psalm 29:10-11).

Isaiah proclaimed,

> *Behold, for peace I had great bitterness: but thou hast in love to my soul delivered it from the pit of corruption: for thou hast cast all my sins behind thy back* (Isaiah 38:17).

Paul wrote,

> *Be careful for nothing; but in every thing by prayer and supplication with thanksgiving let your requests be made known unto God. And the peace of God, which passeth all understanding, shall keep your hearts and minds through Christ Jesus* (Philippians 4:6-7).

The word *"keep"* means "to garrison or guard." The Bible says that the peace of God shall garrison, guard, and protect you.

"The peace of God, which passeth all understanding, shall keep your hearts and minds through Christ Jesus."

If we truly want to give God the glory, we must give God what belongs to Him. Psalm 29:11 says, *"The LORD will bless his people with peace."*

How can we glorify God? When the storms in our lives are raging and there is trouble all around, we can give Him glory by trusting Him for peace. Others see this peace demonstrated in our lives and say, "I cannot understand it. It passes all understanding." In this, the Lord is glorified. How wonderful it is to see Christian people truly live like Christian people. When they do, God gives peace and enables His children to live with peace in their hearts.

The Lord
Is My
Shepherd

"The LORD is my shepherd; I shall not want."

Psalm 23:1

There is no more beautiful piece of literature than the Twenty-third Psalm. The very first expression in this psalm, *"The LORD is my shepherd,"* has calmed troubled hearts for thousands of years. The Lord is my Shepherd. Is He your Shepherd?

Over one thousand times in the Bible, we come upon the words *sheep*, *shepherd*, and *lamb*. Being a sheep is nothing to brag about, but being the Lord's sheep is a wonderful thing.

Sheep are defenseless, dependent animals. There is nothing about a sheep that is brave or courageous. There is nothing about a sheep that is noble or outstanding. There is nothing majestic, grand, or glorious about a sheep. Yet God says we are all sheep. Some are saved sheep and some are lost sheep. Notice that God did not say that we were like lions or eagles, but like defenseless and dependent sheep.

> *He is despised and rejected of men; a man of sorrows, and acquainted with grief: and we hid as it were our faces from him; he was despised, and we esteemed him not. Surely he hath borne our griefs, and carried our sorrows: yet we did esteem him stricken, smitten of God, and afflicted. But he was wounded for our transgressions, he was bruised for our iniquities: the chastisement of our peace was upon him; and with his stripes we are healed. All we*

*like sheep have gone astray; we have turned every
one to his own way; and the LORD hath laid on him
the iniquity of us all* (Isaiah 53:3-6).

You may say, "I do not need Jesus because I am a good person."
But the Bible says, *"All we like sheep have gone astray; we have
turned every one to his own way."* Proverbs 14:12 tells us, *"There is
a way which seemeth right unto a man, but the end thereof are the
ways of death."* Perhaps you have decided that your way is the best
way, the right way. This is the very reason you need Christ. As good
as your way appears to be, it is the way of death and separation from
God forever. We are lost sheep; we need a Shepherd.

The Lord Jesus told three stories to those who gathered near Him.
Sinners came to the Lord Jesus because He loved them. Christ was
criticized greatly by the religious rulers of His day because He
received sinners. In Luke fifteen, we find one of the most beautiful
stories in the Bible. The Bible uses the word *parable*, in the singular,
and gives three stories. We often refer to them as three parables, but
it is actually one parable made up of three stories.

The Lord Jesus began this parable by saying that a certain man
had a hundred sheep. One of them was lost. He left the ninety-nine
that were safe and did everything necessary to find that one lost
sheep. You are that one sheep. I am that one sheep. Jesus Christ is
the Shepherd.

The heart of Christ was deeply moved over people. In the gospel
according to Mark we read,

> *And the apostles gathered themselves together
> unto Jesus, and told him all things, both what they
> had done, and what they had taught. And he said
> unto them, Come ye yourselves apart into a desert
> place, and rest a while: for there were many coming
> and going, and they had no leisure so much as to
> eat. And they departed into a desert place by ship*

> *privately. And the people saw them departing, and many knew him, and ran afoot thither out of all cities, and outwent them, and came together unto him. And Jesus, when he came out, saw much people, and was moved with compassion toward them, because they were as sheep not having a shepherd* (Mark 6:30-34).

Just as the disciples needed rest, Christ needed rest; but when He saw the people, *"He was moved with compassion."* Their hurt entered His heart because He saw them *"as sheep not having a shepherd."*

People need the Shepherd. Because I know *"The LORD is my shepherd,"* I can say *"I shall not want."* When you know the Lord is your Shepherd, you do not have to worry and fret because He has promised to meet every need of your life. When you can say in your heart, *"The LORD is my shepherd,"* then you can also say, *"I shall not want."*

I do not have to worry, wondering if God knows about me because the Lord is my Shepherd. I have absolute assurance that my heavenly Father knows everything I need.

Here we find a trilogy of psalms. This trilogy consists of Psalms 22, 23, and 24. The Holy Spirit placed these psalms together for a purpose. Each has a special message about the Shepherd.

In Psalm 22, we see the Shepherd who went to the cross to bleed and die for us. In Psalm 23, we see the Shepherd who has risen from the dead and provides for all our needs as our ascended Lord, ever living to make intercession for us. In Psalm 24, we see our Shepherd who is the coming King. He is coming again to rule and reign.

God's Word says in Psalm 24,

> *Lift up your heads, O ye gates; and be ye lift up, ye everlasting doors; and the King of glory shall come in. Who is this King of glory? The LORD strong*

and mighty, the LORD mighty in battle. Lift up your heads, O ye gates; even lift them up, ye everlasting doors; and the King of glory shall come in. Who is this King of glory? The LORD of hosts, he is the King of glory. Selah (Psalm 24:7-11).

The Lord Is My Good Shepherd

In Psalm 22, we read of the Good Shepherd who gives His life for the sheep. John 10 sheds more light on this.

The thief cometh not, but for to steal, and to kill, and to destroy: I am come that they might have life, and that they might have it more abundantly. I am the good shepherd: the good shepherd giveth his life for the sheep (John 10:10-11).

Christ came to this earth born of a virgin in Bethlehem's manger, robed in flesh, God incarnate. Mary simply brought forth what God sent forth into the world. The Twenty-third Psalm was a thousand years old when Christ was born in Bethlehem. Mary, who gave birth to the Lord Jesus Christ, more than likely quoted to Him this Twenty-third Psalm.

This passage is one of the first things we memorize from the Bible. *"The LORD is my shepherd; I shall not want."* We also quote this passage when people come to the end of their lives. We find great comfort in the Twenty-third Psalm. *"I will dwell in the house of the LORD for ever."* It is beautiful that the Lord allows us to begin our lives and finish our lives with the same passage of Scripture, the twenty-third Psalm.

When Christ came to earth, He came to bleed and die for our sin. The Good Shepherd gave His life for us on the cross. Why? He died to save us from the *penalty* of sin. Every person who has ever lived and is presently alive is under the penalty of sin. The Bible says in

Romans 3:23, *"For all have sinned, and come short of the glory of God."* We are sinners by conception, we are sinners by choice, and we are sinners by conduct. Whatever sin we commit indicates that we are sinners by nature.

We have sinned, and we must pay. The Bible says in Romans 6:23, *"The wages of sin is death."* The penalty for our sin is death and hell, separation from God forever. Man has no hope of going to heaven until something is done about his sin.

A man may say he is going to be as good as he can be and do what he can to make humanity better. These social concerns may seem to have some value, but all they are doing is making the world a better place from which to go to hell.

We are all sinners hopelessly lost in our sin. The payment of our sin is death and hell. Every man is a lost, condemned sinner and he needs a Savior. The Good Shepherd gave His life to pay our penalty. He died on the cross for our sin.

The Lord Is My Great Shepherd

In Psalm 23, we find the Great Shepherd who lives to meet all our needs and to deliver us not from the penalty of sin–we have already been delivered from the penalty of sin if we have trusted Christ as our Savior–but from the *power* of sin.

The writer of the epistle to the Hebrews tells us,

> *Now the God of peace, that brought again from the dead our Lord Jesus, that great shepherd of the sheep, through the blood of the everlasting covenant, make you perfect in every good work to do his will, working in you that which is wellpleasing in his sight, through Jesus Christ; to whom be glory for ever and ever. Amen* (Hebrews 13:20-21).

What does the Great Shepherd do? As the Good Shepherd, He went to the cross and bled and died for our sin. He was buried in a borrowed tomb and came forth from the grave, alive forevermore. He ascended to heaven and He ever lives to make intercession for us. There He has the ministry of the Great Shepherd, to deliver us from the *power* of sin.

I owed a sin debt, and the Lord Jesus paid the penalty for my sin. Christ Jesus paid it all. Someone may say, "What about the sins I will commit in the future?" All of our sins were future when Jesus Christ died on the cross. He paid for all our sin on Calvary: past, present, and future.

The Devil cannot say, "All right, God, Clarence Sexton still owes a penalty to me. He's a sinner and he must die and go to hell because he still owes a sin debt." When I bowed my unworthy head, asked God to forgive my sin, and trusted Christ as my Savior, I accepted that Christ paid my sin penalty in full. He exchanged records with me. He took my sin upon Himself on the cross, and He imputed His righteousness to my account. I do not owe a penalty to sin. The Good Shepherd paid the penalty.

Christ as the Great Shepherd helps me in dealing with sin and the temptation to sin on a daily basis, delivering me from the power of sin. Life is a struggle. As a Christian, I have two natures, the old and the new. These two natures are always battling one another. We all struggle to be what we should be as children of God.

What help do we have when temptation comes? We brag because we are not guilty of some of the fleshly sins, perhaps sins we were once involved in. It is so much easier to confess other people's sin than to confess our own. If we do not drink alcohol, then everyone who does drink is horrible. If we do not smoke, everyone who does smoke is horrible. If we do not curse, then everyone who does curse is horrible. These things are bad; but all of us are guilty of sins of the spirit, sins that are not so obvious. I would rather have to deal with many drunkards than one gossip. I would rather have to deal with many drunkards than one liar.

What happens when we are tempted to lose our temper, to criticize when we should pray, or to harbor unforgiveness in our hearts when we should forgive? We act like helpless, defenseless sheep without a shepherd. *"The LORD is my shepherd."* If the Lord is our Shepherd, we are not helpless or defenseless. We have a Shepherd to help us deal with the power of sin. We can call on Him, and He will come to our aid. He will help us.

You may be far removed from the Christian life you should be living. Perhaps it is not obvious to other people, but in your heart you know that if you are going to be pleasing to God, you must seek the face of the Lord and ask Him to help you, cleanse you, and forgive you. The flimsy excuses we give for why we have not been the Christians we should be will not stand at the judgment seat of Christ.

In many churches, there is no difference between the lives of those who profess to be Christians and the rest of the world. This is the way people want it. A man who says he is a Christian should be different. How can there be a difference? There can be a difference because we have a Shepherd. The Great Shepherd comes to our aid. He empowers us in the hour of temptation. You may be about to lose your marriage because of sin. You will not be able to look into the faces of your children with peace and a clear conscience if you continue the way you are going. Call on the Great Shepherd! He will give you power to resist temptation and do what you should do. *"The LORD is my Shepherd."* He is my Good Shepherd. He is my Great Shepherd.

The Lord Is My Chief Shepherd

In Psalm 24, we find that the Lord is our Chief Shepherd. He will deliver us from the very *presence* of sin when He comes again. We do not hear enough about the coming of Jesus Christ. He is our victorious King and He is coming again.

The Word of God says in I Peter 2:25 that we need a Shepherd for our souls. *"For ye were as sheep going astray; but are now returned unto the Shepherd and Bishop of your souls."* Who is the Shepherd of our souls?

> *The elders which are among you I exhort, who am also an elder, and a witness of the sufferings of Christ, and also a partaker of the glory that shall be revealed: feed the flock of God which is among you, taking the oversight thereof, not by constraint, but willingly; not for filthy lucre, but of a ready mind; neither as being lords over God's heritage, but being ensamples to the flock* (I Peter 5:1-3).

The pastor is to feed and declare to his flock the things of God. You do not need to go to church and simply hear a review of current events; you can read that for yourself. You need to be in church to hear preaching from God's Word. We need a Shepherd. I Peter 5:4 says, *"And when the chief Shepherd shall appear, ye shall receive a crown of glory that fadeth not away."* The Lord is the Shepherd of our souls.

"The LORD is my shepherd." He is my Good Shepherd. He gave His life for me on the cross. He saved me from the penalty of my sin when I trusted Him as my Savior.

"The LORD is my shepherd." He is my Great Shepherd. He saves me from the power of sin when I call on Him in time of need. He is the risen Savior, sitting at the right hand of God the Father. He is ever living to make intercession for us. Paul wrote in I Timothy 2:5, *"For there is one God, and one mediator between God and men, the man Christ Jesus."* As our Great Shepherd, He gives us the power we need to live the Christian life.

"The LORD is my shepherd." He is my Chief Shepherd. He is my coming King. When He comes again, I will meet Him in the air. He may come today. Are you ready to meet Him?

The psalmist said, *"The LORD is my shepherd; I shall not want."* We can easily say, *"The LORD is my Shepherd."* We find it more difficult to say, *"I shall not want."* Something is wrong in our daily walk with God when we cannot say with confidence, *"I shall not want."*

If we truly know this Shepherd of ours as we should know Him–as the Good Shepherd, the Great Shepherd, and the Chief Shepherd–then we can say with confidence, *"I shall not want."*

He Maketh Me to Lie Down

"He maketh me to lie down in green pastures: he leadeth me beside the still waters."

Psalm 23:2

———————————

he Twenty-third Psalm is called the Psalm of Psalms, the Pearl of the Psalms, and the Shepherd's Psalm. Verse two reads, *"He maketh me to lie down in green pastures."* This verse could be read with the emphasis on the word *"He."* It could be read with the emphasis on the word *"maketh."* It could be read with the emphasis on the word *"me."* But, where should the emphasis be placed? The emphasis should always be on the Shepherd, not on the sheep. The emphasis must be placed on the word *"He." "He maketh me to lie down in green pastures."*

This verse speaks of rest for the sheep. We are His sheep. Our Lord desires for His sheep to rest. In this world, millions do whatever is necessary to take care of their bodies, while starving their souls. Our spirits cry out for the rest that only our Shepherd can provide. The psalmist writes, *"He maketh me to lie down in green pastures."* The word *"maketh"* speaks of yielding to the Shepherd's desire for our lives. The Shepherd provides for us green pastures, and as sheep we are to yield to His placing us in green pastures.

> *Come unto me, all ye that labour and are heavy laden, and I will give you rest. Take my yoke upon you, and learn of me; for I am meek and lowly in heart: and ye shall find rest unto your souls. For my yoke is easy, and my burden is light* (Matthew 11:28-30).

He said, *"I will give you rest."* Then He said, *"Ye shall find rest."* The Bible promises believers three kinds of rest: the rest of salvation, the rest of heaven, and the rest of faith.

THE REST OF SALVATION

We can find rest when we are no longer wrestling as enemies with God, when we have been brought to Him by the blood of Jesus Christ and what He did for us on the cross. Every person who is not a Christian is an enemy of God, unreconciled to God; but the situation is not irreconcilable. Christ went to Calvary where He bled and died for our sins. He paid the sin debt God demanded.

I asked God to forgive my sin and received Christ as my Savior, and my salvation is sure. It is settled forever. God the Father imputed the righteousness of Jesus Christ to my heavenly record. On Calvary He bore my sin. God helping me, I shall never tire of telling people that my sin debt was paid on the cross of Calvary. I can rest because my soul's salvation is in Jesus Christ. For this I do not work because He did all the work on the cross. I simply trust Him. The Word of God says in Ephesians 2:8-9, *"For by grace are ye saved through faith; and that not of yourselves: it is the gift of God: Not of works, lest any man should boast."*

In this world, millions do whatever is necessary to take care of their bodies, while starving their souls.

49

THE REST OF HEAVEN

The Lord Jesus told His disciples that they would find heavenly rest,

Let not your heart be troubled: ye believe in God, believe also in me. In my Father's house are many mansions: if it were not so, I would have told you. I go to prepare a place for you. And if I go and prepare a place for you, I will come again, and receive you unto myself; that where I am, there ye may be also (John 14:1-3).

> *Our public world may be well ordered and defined, but our spirits cry out, "Rest! I need rest."*

Thomas asked in verse five, *"Lord, we know not whither thou goest; and how can we know the way?"* The Lord Jesus answered him in verse six, *"I am the way, the truth, and the life: no man cometh unto the Father, but by me."*

Heaven is my home. I am as sure of it as if I were already there. How can I be so sure? I can be sure because I have God's immutable word on it. You see, God cannot change. He cannot lie, and He said heaven is my eternal home. I do not work for eternal life in heaven; it is a gift I received at the moment Christ came to live within me.

THE REST OF FAITH

There is a third rest that so few Christians seem to enter into, a rest for which we labor. So often the struggle is not with the world, the flesh, and the Devil; the struggle is with God. His sheep must yield to Him. We need to allow Him to place us in the green pastures He has for us.

Matthew 11:28 says, *"Come unto me, all ye that labour and are heavy laden, and I will give you rest."* This is the rest of salvation. Verse twenty-nine continues, *"Take my yoke upon you, and learn of me; for I am meek and lowly in heart: and ye shall find rest unto your souls."* Would you like to find that soul rest, not in the distant future, but now? Would you like to pillow your spirit in the bosom of Jesus Christ and find the sweet peace and rest only He can give? He has provided it. It is ours for the taking by faith, yet we live like orphans. The Shepherd provides this rest by making us to lie down in green pastures.

A portion of Ezekiel 34 has to do with the restoration of Israel and God's provision for them.

> *For thus saith the Lord GOD; Behold, I, even I, will both search my sheep, and seek them out. As a shepherd seeketh out his flock in the day that he is among his sheep that are scattered; so will I seek out my sheep, and will deliver them out of all places where they have been scattered in the cloudy and dark day. And I will bring them out from the people, and gather them from the countries, and will bring them to their own land, and feed them upon the mountains of Israel by the rivers, and in all the inhabited places of the country. I will feed them in a good pasture, and upon the high mountains of Israel shall their fold be: there shall they lie in a good fold, and in a fat pasture shall they feed upon the mountains of Israel. I will feed my flock, and I will cause them to lie down, saith the Lord GOD* (Ezekiel 34:11-14).

This sounds much like Psalm 23:2, *"He maketh me to lie down in green pastures."* He said, *"I will cause them to lie down."*

51

We believers belong to God, and He can do anything He chooses to do with our lives. We must yield our wills to Christ. However, God can bring anything He deems necessary into our lives to cause us to lie down in His green pastures. He knows we need rest for our spirits. Our public world may be well ordered and defined, but our spirits cry out, "Rest! I need rest." Our weary spirits continue to plead for rest until they find the green pastures God has provided for them.

We must always keep our eyes on the Shepherd, not on other sheep. If we are going to have the rest we so desperately need, it will be provided for us by the Shepherd. The Bible says in Psalm 23:1, *"The LORD is my shepherd; I shall not want."* I shall not want for rest because *"He maketh me to lie down in green pastures."*

In order for the sheep to rest, the shepherd must provide certain things for the sheep.

The Fears of the Sheep Are Dealt With by the Shepherd

The shepherd deals with the fears that are common to sheep so they can rest. Sheep are very nervous animals. They can be easily scared by a strange noise, person, or another animal. They are easily frightened. There is only one thing the shepherd can provide that will relieve their fears–his presence. Their fears are not relieved by the removal of danger.

We live in an increasingly perilous world, and we cannot possibly hope to remove every danger or threat. We have all been troubled by the prospect of becoming the victim of a crime or contracting some incurable disease. Remember, the fears of the sheep are not relieved by the absence of danger but by the presence of the shepherd.

The Lord Jesus, our Great Shepherd, comes to our side. In His abiding presence, no matter what is going on around us, He gives rest. It is His presence, even in the presence of danger, that brings peace. When we know that the Shepherd is present, we can rest from our fears.

The Lord Jesus Christ came from heaven to earth to defeat death, hell, and the grave, to conquer every fear. He is the Victor over all. In His earthly ministry, He proved His power over disease–He healed the sick. He proved His power over demons–He cast them out. He proved His power over the Devil–He defeated the Devil and the temptations Satan put before Him. On Calvary, He completed His victory over death, hell, and the grave as He rose from the grave on the third day alive forevermore. In Revelation 1:18 He declared, *"I am he that liveth, and was dead; and, behold, I am alive for evermore, Amen; and have the keys of hell and of death."*

We need rest from our fears. What do you fear? Do you fear a person or circumstance? Do you fear your inability? Do you fear your weakness? We must learn that our fears are not defeated by removing all the things that cause fear. Our fears are defeated by the presence of the Shepherd of our souls.

We cannot rid ourselves of everything in life that may trouble us. However, when we abide in the personal presence of the Shepherd, nothing can harm us without His permission. No, we cannot rest until our fears are calmed. Praise God for the Shepherd who deals with our fears.

The Friction Among the Sheep Is Dealt With by the Shepherd

The shepherd deals with the friction that arises among the sheep. Sheep are contrary animals, much like people. They establish an order among themselves. Chickens have a pecking order. Cattle have a horning order. Among animals, there is an order.

Among sheep, there is a butting order. People who deal with sheep say there may be a ewe lamb, an older female sheep, that takes charge. Any time another sheep is grazing where she wants to graze, she will put her head down and butt the other sheep just to prove she is in charge. This causes an uneasiness among the whole flock. As the sheep become jittery and the friction builds, they cannot rest. When the shepherd arrives on the scene, they stop their butting because they know he is in charge. He deals with the friction that arises among the sheep.

Among God's sheep there is friction, and until it is dealt with, we cannot rest. We are always butting one another. "I don't like what she said." "I don't like what they have." "I don't like how they treated my child." We are always butting. There is always friction. But then the Shepherd steps on the scene. When we consciously abide in the presence of the Shepherd, the friction ceases.

If we leave Christ out of the picture, we can always find a justifiable reason to be irritated with someone or to criticize others. We may become angry with a teacher, a coach, a principal, a pastor, or a family member. There is always the potential for friction.

Families and churches alike have friction when they lack the peace and rest they need. Sheep cannot rest among all this friction. They cannot rest knowing that someone may butt them at any moment.

Do we really want rest? If we do, we must deal with our fears, not by chasing all the danger away, but by living in the presence of the Shepherd. We must deal with our friction, not by making everyone perfect, but by living consciously in the presence of the Shepherd.

The Food Needed by the Sheep Is Provided by the Shepherd

If the sheep are going to rest, they must be fed. The Shepherd provides the food needed by the sheep. *"He maketh me to lie down in green pastures."* He provides nourishment for us in the green pastures He chooses.

Most sheep grazing lands are not found where you might imagine them to be. Most of the great grazing lands are in arid, dry countries where lush, green pastures do not exist. As a matter of fact, if you have ever been to the Middle East and have seen a flock of sheep, you might wonder what they are eating. All that is visible is barren land, rocks, and rough terrain.

It is the shepherd who finds a location where the soil can be cultivated, where rocks can be removed, where the land can be irrigated properly, and where the proper plants can be found. The shepherd knows it is his business to provide the green pastures for his sheep. Not only does he deal with their fears and their friction, but he also knows it is his responsibility to satisfy their need for food.

The fears of the sheep are not relieved by the absence of danger but by the presence of the shepherd.

God has given us a Book that is food for our souls. Yet, God's Word is lying on a coffee table or somewhere in a drawer or on the back seat of an automobile. Jesus Christ has provided this green pasture in which we can graze. No one can see our starving souls because we are well groomed and well dressed. We know just what to say; we have learned all the Christian clichés. But, if our spirits could speak audibly, most would say, "You are starving me!"

The Lord Jesus bridged the gap between God and men at Calvary and made a way that we can go boldly to the throne of grace and talk with God. We can actually call God our Father and abide in sweet communion and prayer with the Lord. He has provided this for us, but we do not graze in it. As a matter of fact, every fiber of our natural man resists grazing there. We want to do everything we can to solve our own problems, to meet our own needs. We are in constant conflict with the old nature about grazing in communion and in prayer with God. May the Lord give us victory in our lives to graze in these green pastures He has provided.

"The Lord is my shepherd; I shall not want. He maketh me to lie down in green pastures." The Shepherd deals with the fears that come to the sheep, the friction that arises among the sheep, and the food needed by the sheep. Because the Shepherd takes care of these things in our lives, we can find sweet rest in His presence.

He Leadeth Me

"He maketh me to lie down in green pastures: he leadeth me beside the still waters."

Psalm 23:2

---

he Twenty-third Psalm is a favorite passage for many of God's children. This passage begins, *"The LORD is my shepherd; I shall not want."* Then the Bible says in verse two, *"He maketh me to lie down in green pastures."* This speaks of rest. The rest we find from fear is not in the absence of danger but in the presence of the Shepherd. May the Lord continue to teach us this lesson because we can be so anxious at times. The cure for our anxiety is not removing the things that cause the anxiety, but entering into the presence of the Shepherd.

Verse two says, *"He maketh me to lie down in green pastures: he leadeth me beside the still waters."* We could read this with emphasis placed on the word *"he,"* the word *"leadeth,"* or the phrase *"still waters."* We are tempted to place the emphasis on *"leadeth"* or *"still waters,"* but again we learn from this psalm that the emphasis should be placed on the Shepherd.

Our Submission to the Shepherd

"He leadeth me beside the still waters." We are not going to be led by the Shepherd unless we submit to the Shepherd. God has established the principle of authority and submission to it.

60

In Isaiah 58:11 the prophet promised, *"And the LORD shall guide thee continually, and satisfy thy soul in drought, and make fat thy bones: and thou shalt be like a watered garden, and like a spring of water, whose waters fail not."* I want my life to be like a watered garden. I love to see a beautiful garden, well-watered and kept. The Lord says our lives can be like a watered garden, but we must allow Him to guide us. *"And the LORD shall guide thee continually."* The psalmist said, *"He leadeth me beside the still waters."*

When our Lord Jesus was about to leave His disciples, He wanted to comfort them. He explained to them the great truth concerning the indwelling Holy Spirit. As our Lord spoke of the Holy Spirit, He said in John 16:7, *"Nevertheless I tell you the truth; It is expedient for you that I go away...."* The word *"expedient"* means "in your best interest." How could it be in their best interest for Christ to leave? The truth is that Christ was not leaving; He was continuing with them in the Person of the Holy Spirit. He said, "I will bleed and die on Golgotha's cross, be buried in a borrowed tomb, come forth from the grave alive, and ascend to heaven. But the Holy Spirit is coming to indwell every believer forever. He will live in you."

We believe that God is coequal, coexistent, and eternally existent in three persons–God the Father, God the Son, and God the Holy Spirit. We understand that God the Son is coequal with God the Father and God the Holy Spirit. God the Holy Spirit is no more or less God than the Father and the Son. God the Son is no more or less God than the Father and the Holy Spirit. God the Father is no more or less God than the Son and the Holy Spirit.

When we speak of the Father, we speak of God. When we speak of the Holy Spirit, we speak of God. When we speak of the Lord Jesus Christ, the Son, we speak of God. This may be a bit difficult to comprehend, but by faith we believe the clear Bible teaching of the Trinity. When we speak of God, we speak of coequal, coexistent, eternally existent God the Father, God the Son, and God the Holy Spirit.

Jesus Christ said, "It is in your best interest that I go away and that the Holy Spirit come to indwell every believer forever." The same Christ who walked with His disciples is abiding in you and in me today and forever in the Person of the Holy Spirit.

In John's gospel record we read the Lord Jesus' promise,

> *...for if I go not away, the Comforter will not come unto you; but if I depart, I will send him unto you. And when he is come, he will reprove the world of sin, and of righteousness, and of judgment: Of sin, because they believe not on me; Of righteousness, because I go to my Father, and ye see me no more; Of judgment, because the prince of this world is judged. I have yet many things to say unto you, but ye cannot bear them now* (John 16:7-12).

The Lord Jesus said, "There is so much I want to teach you, but you can only receive so much at this time." Think of how parents, with dreams of their child one day becoming a wonderful Christian young person will often think, "I'd like to teach him all he needs to know at one time." But it does not work that way. It is a daily process, sometimes a moment-by-moment process. Likewise, as Christians, we grow day by day as we feed on God's Word and commune with Christ our Savior.

He said in verse thirteen, *"Howbeit when he, the Spirit of truth, is come, he will guide you into all truth."* In other words, the Lord Jesus said, "I want to share so many things with you, but you cannot bear them now. When the Holy Spirit comes to live in you, never to leave you or forsake you, He will constantly teach you what you need to know and help you to grow as a believer. The Holy Spirit will guide you."

You may say, "Years ago, I asked God to forgive my sin and by faith I trusted Jesus Christ as my Savior. Years ago, the Lord came to live in me; but I'm not growing as I should grow. I have to admit that." The secret to growing in the Christian life is in yielding to the Shepherd. If He is going to lead us, we must allow Him to lead us. God has established this principle for our lives.

An illustration of this is found in I Timothy 3, where we find the qualifications for both pastors and deacons, the two New Testament offices in the church. God calls and leads a man to a church that believes God has led him to be their pastor. They vote as a church to extend a call to him to be their pastor. This relationship is like a marriage. The church says, "We will love you and we want you to lead us. Will you love us and lead us?" Then the people choose deacons to help that pastor lead the church.

Notice a word in the qualifications listed in I Timothy 3. The Bible says in verse one, *"This is a true saying, If a man desire the office of a bishop, he desireth a good work."* The word *"bishop"* is another word referring to the office of pastor or shepherd.

Continue reading in verse two,

> *A bishop then must be blameless, the husband of one wife, vigilant, sober, of good behaviour, given to hospitality, apt to teach; Not given to wine, no striker, not greedy of filthy lucre; but patient, not a brawler, not covetous; One that ruleth well his own house.*

Notice the word *"ruleth."* This word is too strong for some people, but the Bible clearly says the pastor must *rule* his house. This does not mean he should have his wife and family in chains. He is not to be a tyrant, but he is to lead.

Much of the rebellion in our world today is against what is called the patriarchal society. The root of this patriarchal society, we are told, is the Christian faith. People are in rebellion against God and the Christian faith because they do not think a man should rule. If you are married and you want to have a happy home, you must understand that God's design calls for the husband to lead his family and for his wife to be in submission. This is a principle God has established.

The Scripture continues in verse five, *"For if a man know not how to rule his own house, how shall he take care of the church of God?"* The pastor is to lead the church. The Bible says in I Timothy 5:17, *"Let the elders that rule well be counted worthy of double honour, especially they who labour in the word and doctrine."* The word *elder* is another word for pastor. God calls a pastor to lead a church. A church should be pastor-led. Not every church believes this, but Baptist people who believe the Bible believe that under Christ a pastor should lead the church.

This is not said for the pastor's sake or for the husband's sake; but to teach a principle, a principle of authority and submission to authority. Think of what God could do for us if only we were willing to be submissive!

Happiness is a by-product of obedience. You will never be a happy wife unless you are submissive to your husband's leadership. You will never be a happy husband unless you submit to Christ and to the needs of your wife. I will never be a happy pastor if I do not lead the church and submit to the needs of the church. We will not be what God wants us to be unless we are submissive to authority.

In order for our Shepherd to lead us, we must be submissive to His will for our lives. Who knows more about our lives than the Shepherd? Do we know more about our lives, or does God know more about our lives? Who knows more about why we were created? Why do we make such disasters of our lives? Because we try to run our own lives. Why do we cause such heartache in the lives of others? Because we try to manage our own lives. We say, "I'm going to be my own boss. No one will rule over me." But we must come to a place of submission if we expect our Shepherd to lead us. Everything else in life is settled when this is settled.

Our battle is not with people; it is with yielding to Christ. A woman may say, "I'm battling my husband." The real struggle is your unwillingness to be submissive to God and the person God has placed in your life. A husband may say, "I'm battling my wife and kids." Examine your life to see if the real struggle may be that you have not yielded yourself to God to be the husband and father God wants you to be.

If God is going to lead us, we must submit to Him. We must be in submission to the Shepherd.

Our Supply From the Shepherd

"He leadeth me beside the still waters." Life without water is impossible, and He supplies us with the water we need.

Almost seventy percent of a sheep's body consists of water. Water is necessary for every bodily function. If the sheep does not get the water he needs, his body will not function properly.

It is not up to the sheep to find the water. Sheep have no sense of direction. The Shepherd must lead the sheep to *"the still waters."* These are still waters, not raging streams that can take the life of the sheep. *"He leadeth me beside the still waters."*

The shepherd provides three sources of water for the sheep. One source is a deep well where the shepherd finds water for the sheep. At times the shepherd must work with great effort to get the water to the sheep from the deep well. Many times God takes us to the deep well, and our Shepherd works tirelessly to get the water to us. It may look like a dark, troubled place, a place where it seems no water can be found; but He knows that in that deep well there is water for us, and He takes us to it.

Water is also found in streams and springs. The sheep can drink freely from the cool, refreshing water found there.

Another source of water for the sheep is dew. I am told that sheep can go for prolonged periods of time and never drink from a well or from a stream or spring if they can get enough dew. In the very early morning, dew can be found on the vegetation. The sheep can eat the lush vegetation covered in dew and find all the water they need. To get that water, they must arrive early in the morning before the heat of the day burns off the dew. The shepherd must take them to find a place to graze where the dew can be found upon the lush vegetation. Early in the day, before the heat of the sun, he leads the sheep to the place where they can walk among the dew-covered grass and vegetation and get the water they need.

What can we learn from this? It is not the sheep but the Shepherd who leads us to our supply. What is the water for our lives? The Bible says in John 7:37, *"In the last day, that great day of the feast, Jesus stood and cried, saying, If any man thirst...."* Thirst is a gift from God. The sheep know their bodies need water because they get thirsty.

We have physical thirst, and sometimes we quench that thirst with things that are not hydrating, but dehydrating. We consume many liquids that are not hydrating liquids. They do not provide water for us; they actually take water from our bodies. By drinking these liquids, we have more water removed from our bodies.

In our spiritual life, God gives us thirst. So often, we try to quench that thirst with "dehydrating" things instead of "hydrating" things. They seem to satisfy, but in the end they do not satisfy. They actually harm us.

The Lord Jesus said, *"If any man thirst, let him come unto me, and drink."* What does *"drink"* mean in this verse? *"Drink"* is another word for "accept, believe, or take."

In John 4, we find the beautiful story of the woman at the well. This woman had been married five times and was presently living with a man in adultery. Her life was wrecked. She went to the well at noonday to draw water. She went at noonday because she knew the other women would be gone. She did not want to be embarrassed by the presence of the other women in the village. But Christ had an appointment to meet her at the well. The Lord Jesus saw her thirsty soul and spoke directly to her deepest need.

> *But whosoever drinketh of the water that I shall give him shall never thirst; but the water that I shall give him shall be in him a well of water springing up into everlasting life. The woman saith unto him, Sir, give me this water, that I thirst not, neither come hither to draw. Jesus saith unto her, Go, call thy husband, and come hither. The woman answered and said, I have no husband. Jesus said unto her, Thou hast well said, I have no husband: For thou hast had five husbands; and he whom thou now hast is not thy husband: in that saidst thou truly* (John 4:14-18).

How we need the heart Christ has for people! We are so full of hypocrisy. We make a practice of finding sins we do not commit and lifting our voices against others who do those things. The Bible says in John 3:16, *"For God so loved the world that He gave His only begotten Son."* I am *against* sin, but God help me to be *for* sinners the way I should be for sinners. I am against sin, and you should be against sin; but may we have the love of Christ for people.

The wonderful story of grace continues,

> *The woman saith unto him, Sir, I perceive that thou art a prophet. Our fathers worshipped in this mountain; and ye say, that in Jerusalem is the place where men ought to worship. Jesus saith unto her, Woman, believe me, the hour cometh, when ye shall neither in this mountain, nor yet at Jerusalem, worship the Father. Ye worship ye know not what: we know what we worship: for salvation is of the Jews. But the hour cometh, and now is, when the true*

worshippers shall worship the Father in spirit and in truth: for the Father seeketh such to worship him. God is a Spirit: and they that worship him must worship him in spirit and in truth. The woman saith unto him, I know that Messias cometh, which is called Christ: when he is come, he will tell us all things. Jesus saith unto her, I that speak unto thee am he (John 4:19-26).

Some say the Lord Jesus never claimed to be the Messiah. They do not know the Bible. The woman said, *"I know that Messias cometh."* Christ Jesus said, *"I that speak unto thee am he."* How much clearer could He be? Either Christ is the promised Messiah, or He lied to that woman. God cannot lie. It is not that He does not lie, but He cannot lie.

The woman received eternal water by believing on Him. *"The LORD is my shepherd; I shall not want. He maketh me to lie down in green pastures: he leadeth me beside the still waters."* The water we need for life, for spiritual existence, comes from believing Christ.

Our Satisfaction From the Shepherd

To be satisfied, the sheep must drink. People often say to me, "I know that. I've heard that before. I believe that." But their souls will not be satisfied until they take it, until they drink, until they believe the Lord, until they go to the water and take it in. For every clear, cool drink God has for us, the Devil rushes up with something else to try to satisfy us. Only the Lord Jesus can truly satisfy.

The sheep traveled through places where there were holes dug out in the earth. As they walked through the water, they excreted their own waste into the water, and mud was mingled in the water. That was not the kind of water the shepherd wanted the sheep to drink. He did not want them to drink water that could harm them. He wanted them to drink clear, cool, refreshing water.

Our Lord does not want us to drink water contaminated with the things of this world. He desires for us to satisfy our spiritual thirsts with the clear, cool drink of heaven He has for us.

The Bible says in the book of Jeremiah that God has two things against His people. Jeremiah 2:13 says, *"For my people have committed two evils...."* What are they? The first one, *"...they have forsaken me the fountain of living waters...."* Christ is the Fountain of living waters. There is no other place to get living water. The Shepherd will lead us every day to drink if we will let Him. We will never be satisfied with anything else.

He said, "The first evil is that they have forsaken Me, the Fountain of living waters." Then He said, *"...and hewed them out cisterns, broken cisterns, that can hold no water."* In other words, "They tried to create places to get water. They have hewn out places to catch and hold water, but they are broken and cannot hold water."

Remember, about seventy percent of a sheep's body consists of water. All the functions of the animal's body depend on that water. Do you know why so many of us who say we are Christians are not functioning like Christians? We are not getting the water from the Shepherd so that we can function the way His sheep should function. We have hewn out or created places where we can get a drink, but the water found there is not fit for consumption. Yet, we continue to drink it.

For every clear, cool drink God has for us, the Devil rushes up with something else to try to satisfy us.

Often people look at Bible-believing Christians and say, "You are radical, off-the-wall. All you talk about is straight living!" What do we need? We need God to divide us, to discern for us, to separate us from all the unfit water and lead us to drink what He has prepared for us.

Our souls need to be fed from the fountains, streams, springs, deep wells, and early morning dew that Christ Jesus provides. We need to get it early in the morning before the heat of the day burns the water away. Why go through every day with a parched soul when we can be refreshed early from the presence of the Lord?

"The LORD is my shepherd; I shall not want. He maketh me to lie down in green pastures: he leadeth me beside the still waters."

He Restoreth My Soul

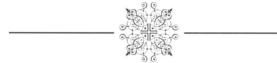

"He restoreth my soul: he leadeth me in the paths of righteousness for his name's sake."

Psalm 23:3

"T*he LORD is my shepherd; I shall not want."* He is not *the* Shepherd, not *a* Shepherd, but *my* Shepherd. When this is the testimony of our lives, then we will also be able to say, *"I shall not want"* because we will know that our Shepherd provides everything we need.

The Bible says in Psalm 23:2, *"He maketh me to lie down in green pastures: he leadeth me beside the still waters."* We have considered these phrases found in the Twenty-third Psalm. We come now to the third verse where the Bible says, *"He restoreth my soul."*

We must keep our eyes on the Shepherd, not on the sheep. Every fear in life will vanish if we keep our eyes on the Shepherd. The rest we need as sheep is not found in the absence of all danger. Our rest is found in the presence of the Shepherd. We learn this in life as the Lord Jesus comes to us in our great hour of need. We can rest in Him.

The Bible says, *"He restoreth my soul."* Emphasis could be placed on the word *"restoreth,"* or the word *"soul,"* but we should place the emphasis on the Shepherd. *"He restoreth my soul."* This is the only way our souls can be restored.

The Bible says in Psalm 42:1-5,

> *As the hart panteth after the water brooks, so panteth my soul after thee, O God. My soul thirsteth*

for God, for the living God: when shall I come and appear before God? My tears have been my meat day and night, while they continually say unto me, Where is thy God? When I remember these things, I pour out my soul in me: for I had gone with the multitude, I went with them to the house of God, with the voice of joy and praise, with a multitude that kept holyday. Why art thou cast down, O my soul? and why art thou disquieted in me? hope thou in God: for I shall yet praise him for the help of his countenance.

Notice the word *"cast"* in verse five. In old English, shepherds would speak of a sheep that was *cast*, meaning the sheep was on his back in a helpless, frightened position and could not get up. Perhaps the sheep was looking for a soft place to lie in the grass and fell over too far one way, or perhaps the sheep weighed too much and fell over onto his back. This is a dangerous position. If the sheep stayed in that position long, he could die. In the *cast* position the sheep is defenseless and lacks the ability to flee from animals that would prey on him.

Here the psalmist said, *"Why art thou cast down?"* He was saying, "Why do you feel that you are in a helpless position? Why do you think you are vulnerable to anything that may come to destroy you?" Verse five says, *"Why art thou disquieted in me? hope thou in God: for I shall yet praise him for the help of his countenance."*

The sheep that was cast down needed to be restored. When David prayed in Psalm 51:12, he said, *"Restore unto me the joy of thy salvation."* He did not say, "Restore unto me Thy salvation."

We should distinguish between the two words, *relationship* and *fellowship*. We establish the right relationship with Jesus Christ when we come to know Him as our Savior and He comes to live in us.

> *My sheep hear my voice, and I know them, and they follow me: And I give unto them eternal life; and they shall never perish, neither shall any man pluck them out of my hand. My Father, which gave them me, is greater than all; and no man is able to pluck them out of my Father's hand* (John 10:27-29).

Our relationship with Jesus Christ is something that cannot be changed. Once we are born into God's family by faith, we cannot be unborn. We have *"eternal life,"* and this life begins the moment we trust Christ as Savior. We are saved by His precious blood. The Lord Jesus came to this earth and lived a sinless life. At Calvary, He took upon Himself the sins of the whole world. He bled and died for our sins, not His own. Our holy God said that sin must be paid for, and God's Son, the Lord Jesus, said, "I'll pay the sin debt." When He bore our sins in His body on the cross, the holiness of God was satisfied with Christ's death for our sins. The payment was made by the blood of the Lord Jesus. He was buried in a borrowed tomb, and He came forth from the grave, alive forevermore. The resurrection is God's receipt for the payment made by the blood of Christ.

When we ask God to forgive our sin and trust in what Christ did for us on the cross, the Lord Jesus comes to live in us. He promised in Revelation 3:20, *"Behold, I stand at the door, and knock: if any man hear my voice, and open the door, I will come in to him."* He knocked at my heart's door and I willingly said, "Lord, come in." He came in.

Once He comes in, the Bible says He will never leave us or forsake us. Our relationship with Him cannot be changed. We cannot be children of God one day and the next day be children of the Devil. Once we become children of God, we are born into His family eternally.

We know that God's work is greater than Satan's work because Satan's work can be undone but God's work of salvation can never be undone.

Fellowship is what we have in common. All of God's children should daily be in communion with Christ, be in fellowship with Him, because we can lose this sweet fellowship. David did not pray, "Restore unto me Thy salvation." He prayed, *"Restore unto me the joy of thy salvation...."* It was not his salvation that was gone; it was his joy that was gone. Then David said, *"...and uphold me with thy free spirit."* In other words, "Lord, keep me upright." As a sheep, lying on his back in a helpless position, the shepherd would come and turn over the sheep, placing him in an upright position.

Our Opportunities Can Be Restored

The word *"restore"* means "to bring again" or "to bring home." Studying the word *"restore"* in the Bible, we find that our opportunities can be restored. You may feel as if you have ruined things, as if nothing good will ever come your way again. You may feel that you have made a wreck of your life and your family and that nothing good can ever be restored.

In Joel 2, God spoke to His people Israel. He said in verse twenty-five, *"And I will restore to you the years that the locust hath eaten, the cankerworm, and the caterpillar, and the palmerworm, my great army which I sent among you."* Pay special attention to the word *"restore."*

God said, "I've judged you with the locust, the cankerworm, the caterpillar, and the palmerworm. You have been judged because of your sin, but I will restore to you the years." Does that mean God could make them live those years over again? No, the Lord was saying, "With the life you have left, I am going to restore everything you have lost."

Are you happy? Are you joyful in the Lord? You say, "I'm not as joyful as I could be." God can restore. The Lord can work in your life to make so much of what you have left that it far exceeds your losses.

Others Can Be Restored

In Galatians 6:1, Paul wrote, *"Brethren, if a man be overtaken in a fault, ye which are spiritual, restore such an one in the spirit of meekness; considering thyself, lest thou also be tempted."*

Christians give evidence of their spiritual maturity when they seek to restore the fallen. It should be the natural work of the body of Christ to restore people. We prove that we are not spiritually mature Christians when we do not seek to restore others.

"I will restore to you the years that the locust hath eaten..."

When there are people among us who know the Lord but choose to stray into sin, God tells us that we should restore them. We are to bring them back. When there is sin, there should be repentance and forgiveness; but it does not stop there. There must also be restoration. We must work at restoring people, bringing them back, treating them as if they had never sinned, and doing all we can to show the love of Christ.

Our Souls Can Be Restored

Everything we have dealt with thus far depends on the restoring of our souls. There is something at the very heart of the matter for which there can be no substitute. When we come into proper communion with Christ, when our own souls are restored and we are in fellowship with the Lord, He completely changes our lives.

You may have wounds from which you think you can never recover. However, you can be healed of any wound if your soul is restored.

The psalmist said, *"The LORD is my shepherd; I shall not want. He maketh me to lie down in green pastures: he leadeth me beside the still waters. He restoreth my soul."* He brings us back where we should be.

The sheep does not restore himself; this is the work of the Shepherd. The Shepherd is constantly working to restore us. We are not able to do with opportunities or with others what we should until we allow God to do a work of grace in our own souls. *"He restoreth my soul."*

We find a very clear story in the New Testament of the Shepherd restoring one of His sheep. The Lord Jesus is the Shepherd, and Simon Peter is the sheep. Peter had bragged, "If You are betrayed, no matter what it costs, I'm going to stand with You. I'll give my life for You if it comes to that!" However, before the cock crew, just as Christ had said, Peter swore with an oath, denying that he even knew the Lord. This was a man who walked with Christ, who was one of His own.

Just how was Peter restored? In Luke 22, the Shepherd went about restoring His sheep.

PETER WAS LOVED BY THE LORD

If we have proven to people that we love them, we can go to them in their time of greatest need and they will listen because they know we love them. The Lord Jesus proved to Peter that He loved him long before Peter denied his Lord. Peter was somewhere watching as Christ bled and died upon the cross. And wherever he was, there was no doubt in Peter's mind that the Lord Jesus loved him.

We are loved by the Lord Jesus Christ with an everlasting love. This means that there was never a time when God did not love us. This means there was never a time God started loving us and there will never be a time when He will stop loving us. He is eternal and He loves us with an everlasting love.

PETER WAS PRAYED FOR BY THE LORD

The Lord Jesus said in Luke 22:31-32, *"Simon, Simon, behold, Satan hath desired to have you, that he may sift you as wheat: But I have prayed for thee."*

The failures in my personal life are prayer failures. The failures in my family life are prayer failures. I have talked to my children far more than I have prayed for them. I have prayed for them every day, but I have talked too much and prayed too little.

The Lord Jesus is constantly praying for us. He said to Peter, *"I have prayed for thee."* The sheep that needs to be brought back by the Shepherd is going to be restored because the Shepherd loves him and the Shepherd prays for him. The Word of God says, *"He restoreth my soul."*

PETER WAS CALLED FOR BY NAME

In Mark 16:7, after the resurrection of Christ, the divine messenger was sent with this message, *"But go your way, tell his disciples and Peter that he goeth before you into Galilee: there shall ye see him, as he said unto you."* He called Peter by name. He singled him out.

We have the idea that there are so many people who claim to be Christians, so many sheep in God's fold, that some are overlooked. However, God knows each of us by name. He has the hairs of our heads numbered. He knows all about us.

Peter was called for by name. When the Holy Spirit deals with you through the preaching of God's Word, there may be hundreds of people in the meeting, but you know the Spirit of God is calling for you by name. The Lord Jesus knows your name, and by His Spirit He is saying, "I want you to be restored to Me. I love you. I pray for you. I want you to be near Me."

PETER'S SIN WAS SEEN BY CHRIST

In Luke 22, Peter spoke with an oath denying that he knew Christ. The Bible says in verse sixty-one, *"And the Lord turned, and looked upon Peter. And Peter remembered the word of the Lord, how he had said unto him, Before the cock crow, thou shalt deny me thrice."* Peter's sin was seen by the Lord.

A vital part of the Shepherd's restoration of the sheep takes place when the sheep realizes the Shepherd has seen his sin. When the piercing eyes of Jesus Christ met the eyes of Peter, when Peter denied that he knew the Lord, Peter *"went out and wept bitterly."* As Peter looked toward Christ, the Lord Jesus was looking at Peter. His eyes are always on us. The moment we look to the Savior, we realize He has always been looking at us.

May God by His Holy Spirit speak to us and help us to know that He sees our sin and waits for us to receive His forgiveness as we confess our sins.

PETER WAS ABLE TO REMEMBER HIS SIN

Days had passed since Peter denied the Lord, and the disciples went fishing and caught nothing. They had been fishing all night, and as the sun rose, they could see the silhouette of Someone on the shore of Galilee. It was the Lord Jesus. When they reached the shore, Christ had prepared breakfast for them. Just as Peter denied the Lord Jesus three times, Christ questioned him three times, causing Peter to remember his sin. God has given us the capacity to remember our unconfessed sin. This is not punishment but a part of the process of restoration.

PETER HAD TO FACE THE HEART OF THE MATTER

The Lord Jesus asked Peter three times, *"Lovest thou me?"* This question put the issue right where it needed to be placed. If we are going to be restored in our fellowship with the Lord and be able to say as the psalmist said, *"He restoreth my soul,"* then we must face the real heart of the issue.

Peter had bragged in front of everyone, "If everyone denies You, You can count on me." He was full of himself. We all have a real problem with pride. However, it goes deeper than that. Christ said, "Here is the great question, Peter. Do you love Me?" The real heart of the matter is loving Jesus Christ.

We all know someone who got involved in the wrong thing. Before that happened, something took place in his daily walk with God. There was a failure in his personal walk with God before something happened that everyone could see.

At the heart of the issue is whether or not we love the Lord. You may say, "I can't get along with this person." That is not the problem. When our souls are restored, we can deal with others. When our souls are restored, we can deal with the opportunities God gives us. We cannot deal with others and with opportunities until first our souls are restored and we are in communion with Christ.

Consider how far Peter could have gone away from God if the Shepherd had not gone after him. He is after you. If you are going to help anyone else, you must first allow God to deal with your own heart.

In the Twenty-third Psalm, David testifies as a sheep praising his Shepherd. Because the Lord is my Shepherd, *"I shall not want."* Because the Lord is my Shepherd, *"He leadeth me beside the still waters."* Because the Lord is my Shepherd, *"He maketh me to lie down in green pastures."* Because the Lord is my Shepherd, *"He restoreth my soul."*

For His Name's Sake

"He restoreth my soul: he leadeth me in the paths of righteousness for his name's sake."

Psalm 23:3

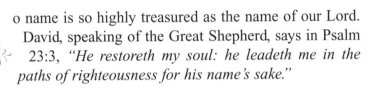 o name is so highly treasured as the name of our Lord. David, speaking of the Great Shepherd, says in Psalm 23:3, *"He restoreth my soul: he leadeth me in the paths of righteousness for his name's sake."*

Because the Shepherd cares for His sheep, He leads them *"in the paths of righteousness for his name's sake."* The psalmist sees himself, not as a shepherd, but as a lamb led by the Shepherd.

Most often, we think of a sheep as being a rather helpless creature. David was a man of war and valor; he was a man's man. He could hold his own in any fight.

There were at the same time things that were beautiful in the life of David–his singing, his writing, and his playing of the harp. David possessed a beauty about his life that was a wonderful thing to behold, but there was nothing lacking in his manhood. He had learned the great lesson in life that we do not live by force but by faith. David was content to be a little lamb led by the Great Shepherd.

We know that sheep have no sense of direction. When they are lost, they cannot find their way; they need someone to lead them. When they are dirty, they have no means to clean themselves; someone must clean them.

We are like sheep. The Bible says in Isaiah 53:6, *"All we like sheep have gone astray; we have turned every one to his own way; and the LORD hath laid on him the iniquity of us all."* Like those sheep, we cannot clean ourselves, and like those sheep, we cannot find the right path when we have turned to our own way. We need someone to show us *"the paths of righteousness."*

If you do not like the idea of being referred to as a sheep, remember that the Great Shepherd became a lamb, a sacrificial lamb. He had things said of Him that we have never had said of us. He had things done to Him that we have never had and never shall have done to us. He is the Lamb of God slain from the foundation of the world. He bled and died for our sins. The Great Shepherd became a lamb yielding to angry men as they did with Him as they pleased.

When we think of our pride, our unwillingness to be yielded, may God help us to think of what Christ did in yielding Himself for us. The Word of God says in Psalm 23:1-3,

> *The LORD is my shepherd; I shall not want. He maketh me to lie down in green pastures: he leadeth me beside the still waters. He restoreth my soul: he leadeth me in the paths of righteousness for his name's sake.*

The Shepherd Has a Plan

The Shepherd leads us *"in the paths of righteousness for his name's sake."* The shepherd has a plan. He is conscious at all times of the needs of the sheep–where they need to go, what they need to eat, what they need to drink. His life is given to the sheep. Can you imagine how foolish an idea it would be for the sheep to attempt to lead the shepherd or for a sheep to attempt to lead the other sheep? They must have a shepherd to lead them.

Just as foolish as it is to think of a lowly sheep leading a shepherd, it is foolish for us to think that we can lead our own lives. The real struggle is allowing God to lead us, admitting that we have lost our way, admitting that we need our Shepherd, the Lord Jesus, to lead us.

We know that our sins are forgiven. We know that Christ paid our sin debt on the cross. We have asked Him to forgive our sin and by faith received Him as our Savior. But, many of us are not allowing Him to lead. The Shepherd says in the psalm that He leads the sheep. The sheep declares, *"He leadeth me."*

In Isaiah 58:11 the Bible says,

> *And the* LORD *shall guide thee continually, and satisfy thy soul in drought, and make fat thy bones: and thou shalt be like a watered garden, and like a spring of water, whose waters fail not.*

In this one verse, there are four things the Lord does as He guides us. *He satisfies our soul in drought.* When we cannot find satisfaction, God can satisfy us. There is a deep longing in all of us that cannot be satisfied apart from Christ. Have you found Him to be not just your Savior, but your Satisfier? Oh, how He satisfies!

The Lord not only satisfies, but the Bible says in the same verse that *He makes fat our bones.* He is speaking of the health of the bones. If you do not have healthy bones, you do not have a healthy body. In the marrow of our bones, we have the factory that produces our blood. If that marrow is not healthy, we cannot be healthy. The psalmist says that as we allow the Lord to lead us, He keeps us healthy and strong in Him.

Notice what else the Lord says. We are like a *"watered garden."* You can labor to put out a garden, till the soil, plant the crop, but if it is not watered, it is not going to grow. Many folks work themselves to exhaustion, but there is no growth. When we do not allow Him to lead us, we are like the little dog trying to catch his own tail, going round and round. We are like the New Yorker who said, "I dig the ditch to get the money to get the food to get the strength to dig the ditch. Then I go dig the ditch to get the money to get the food to get the strength to dig the ditch." Around and around he goes.

You may be everlastingly at it, but the water is not there to make your life grow, to make it beautiful. God says, "You let Me guide you, and I will keep the water coming. You will be like a *watered garden*." He says, "As far as the water is concerned, you will be like *"a spring of water whose waters fail not."* There will always be water available when He guides us.

The Bible says in Psalm 31:3, *"For thou art my rock and my fortress; therefore for thy name's sake lead me, and guide me."* He is our rock and fortress, and He longs to lead us for His glory.

Many of the stories in Scripture deal with God leading people. Most of us are familiar with the story of God leading the children of Israel out of Egyptian bondage and along the path that He chose for them. He led them to the Red Sea. When they came to the Red Sea, they could not pass through.

Why did God lead them this way? Why did He lead them to a place where they could not go, where Moses had to say in Exodus 14:13, *"Stand still, and see the salvation of the LORD"?*

The people would not have chosen to go this way, but it was not their choice to make. The direction God has for us is not our choice to make; it is our choice to give our lives to God and leave the leading to Him.

God led them this way so He could prove Himself to them and be glorified in the path that He had chosen for them.

As we look at what we go through in life, what we deal with on a daily basis, and what has come to us, we must see that God wants to lead us in a way where He can prove Himself to us.

The Shepherd Has a Place

The place the Shepherd has chosen for us is *"the paths of righteousness."* What does *"in the paths of righteousness"* mean?

The sheep walk the same path again and again and wear it down until there is no grass on which to graze. Finally, it becomes a rut. After the rain comes, the rut becomes a muddy trough. Unsanitary conditions and disease set up in this rut due to the excrement of the sheep. The sheep unwittingly wade through the diseased rut endangering themselves. The shepherd must choose another path for them because the path they choose for themselves is a harmful one. We can see what God intends here, can we not?

We choose the ruts of life for ourselves, and we call these ruts "safe places." We are familiar with them. We do not want to move anywhere else, do anything else, or be pushed anywhere else because we have our path, our rut. We do not need to trust God anymore because of our familiarity. We live in this rut if we can, but that is not what God chooses for us. The Shepherd chooses a path of righteousness.

Let us consider these *"paths of righteousness."* Listen as wisdom cries out.

> *The fear of the LORD is to hate evil: pride, and arrogancy, and the evil way, and the froward mouth, do I hate. Counsel is mine, and sound wisdom: I am understanding; I have strength. By me kings reign, and princes decree justice. By me princes rule, and nobles, even all the judges of the earth. I love them that love me; and those that seek me early shall find me. Riches and honour are with me; yea, durable riches and righteousness. My fruit is better than gold, yea, than fine gold; and my revenue than choice silver. I lead in the way of righteousness, in*

*the midst of the paths of judgment: That I may cause
those that love me to inherit substance; and I will fill
their treasures* (Proverbs 8:13-21).

God said, *"I lead in the way of righteousness, in the midst of the
paths of judgment."* Why does God lead us *"in the way of
righteousness"?* He says, *"That I may cause those that love me to
inherit substance; and I will fill their treasures."* God says, "I am
going to lead you in a path that I choose for you, the plan I have for
your life. You must walk by faith and follow Me." All along this
path, God places treasures for us–wonderful things, great joys
and blessings.

Often I think of people who are trying to find a life's mate. They
do not need to try to find a life's mate; they need to follow the path
God has chosen for them. If they follow the Lord, He will bring into
their life the husband or wife that He desires for them.

We place far too much emphasis on finding things and too little
emphasis on following the Lord. The Lord wants us to follow Him
on *"the paths of righteousness"* and allow Him to bless us with
treasures. The Lord speaks of things that money cannot
buy–blessings, peace of heart, provision, friendships, and people
who love us. If we stop and think, we will realize God has allowed
people to cross our paths that are worth far more than silver and gold.

Our Lord has already seen the path. He knows the way. He knows
where it leads. We do not have to know the beginning from the end.
All we must do is follow Him. He puts us on *"the paths of
righteousness."* As we walk these paths of righteousness, He leaves
us substance and treasure. Keep walking. Keep following.

We read in Psalm 5:1-8,

> *Give ear to my words, O LORD, consider my
> meditation. Hearken unto the voice of my cry, my
> King, and my God: for unto thee will I pray. My
> voice shalt thou hear in the morning, O LORD; in the*

morning will I direct my prayer unto thee, and will look up. For thou art not a God that hath pleasure in wickedness: neither shall evil dwell with thee. The foolish shall not stand in thy sight: thou hatest all workers of iniquity. Thou shalt destroy them that speak leasing: the LORD will abhor the bloody and deceitful man. But as for me, I will come into thy house in the multitude of thy mercy: and in thy fear will I worship toward thy holy temple. Lead me, O LORD, in thy righteousness because of mine enemies; make thy way straight before my face.

He not only puts us on the path, but He enables us to stay on the path. We can continue, not in our own strength, but in His strength. I cannot live the victorious Christian life in my own strength. I can live it only through Him and through His enabling. He puts me on the path, and He expects me to stay on it and to trust Him for the strength to stay on this path.

I grew up in Maryville, Tennessee, in the foothills of the Great Smoky Mountains. From time to time we would hear stories of someone getting lost in the mountains. I remember one such story about a little boy who was on an outing with his family. When the boy was discovered to be missing, people immediately assembled to begin a search. At one point, thousands of people were searching for him. Dogs were sniffing for his scent trying to find him. Helicopters flew overhead. Every kind of effort imaginable was made to find the boy.

If you have ever been on any of the paths in those woods, you know the paths are well marked; they are well worn. They are easy to see. But just off the path, the undergrowth is so thick that one can hardly see anything off the path. It is as black as night just a little way off the path.

After all the intense searching, the boy could not be found. When the mother was asked how this could have happened, she said, "He got off the path. That is all I remember. He got off the path. We were all together as a family, walking the path, and just for a moment, he got off the path. Now we can't find him."

How many people do you know who are missing because they decided for a moment to get off the path? They did not know how far they would go or where it would lead them, but they just barely got off the path. God says, "The enemy is out there. You need to follow Me to stay on the path of righteousness." May God help us to do that.

The Shepherd Has a Purpose

The Shepherd has a plan, *"he leadeth me."* He has a path for us to walk, *"the paths of righteousness."* The Shepherd has a purpose. The purpose is *"for his name's sake."*

This expression, *"for his name's sake,"* is used often in the Bible. It means for God to be glorified in the way we live. It means for us to praise the Lord and give Him glory in the way we live, honoring Him.

You remember the story of David and Goliath. David came upon the scene where the armies of Israel encamped on one side of the Valley of Elah and the armies of the Philistines on the other side. For days, the Philistine giant came down, blasphemed God and cursed the people of Israel by the names of the Philistine gods. Finally, David came upon the scene and said, "I can't take that loud mouth talking about God that way." His brother said, "You little runt, whose keeping those *'few sheep in the wilderness'*? We know why you are here. You're out here to see the battle." And David answered, *"Is there not a cause?"*

Soon word reached Saul that someone was willing to fight the giant, Goliath. He was thrilled until he saw David. Saul said to David, *"Thou art but a youth, and he a man of war from his youth."* But David spoke to Saul saying,

> *Thy servant kept his father's sheep, and there came a lion, and a bear, and took a lamb out of the flock: And I went out after him, and smote him, and delivered it out of his mouth: and when he arose against me, I caught him by his beard, and smote him, and slew him. Thy servant slew both the lion and the bear: and this uncircumcised Philistine shall be as one of them, seeing he hath defied the armies of the living God. David said moreover, The LORD that delivered me out of the paw of the lion, and out of the paw of the bear, he will deliver me out of the hand of this Philistine. And Saul said unto David, Go, and the LORD be with thee* (I Samuel 17:34-37).

David was so convincing that the king said, *"The LORD be with thee,"* as if Saul were trusting the Lord.

David went with a sling. The Philistine giant came down and said to David in I Samuel 17:43-46,

> *Am I a dog, that thou comest to me with staves? And the Philistine cursed David by his gods. And the Philistine said to David, Come to me, and I will give thy flesh unto the fowls of the air, and to the beasts of the field. Then said David to the Philistine, Thou comest to me with a sword, and with a spear, and with a shield: but I come to thee in the name of the LORD of hosts, the God of the armies of Israel, whom thou hast defied. This day will the LORD deliver thee into mine hand; and I will smite thee, and take thine head from thee; and I will give the carcases of the host of the Philistines this day unto the fowls of the air, and to the wild beasts of the earth; that all the earth may know that there is a God in Israel.*

Do you know how God wants us to live? He wants us to live in such a way and walk in such a way that His name is lifted up. We are not doing that. Our nation is not doing that. Our churches are not doing that. Listen to what the Lord said of His own people, Israel.

> *Moreover the word of the LORD came unto me, saying, Son of man, when the house of Israel dwelt in their own land, they defiled it by their own way and by their doings: their way was before me as the uncleanness of a removed woman. Wherefore I poured my fury upon them for the blood that they had shed upon the land, and for their idols wherewith they had polluted it: And I scattered them among the heathen, and they were dispersed through the countries: according to their way and according to their doings I judged them. And when they entered unto the heathen, whither they went, they profaned my holy name, when they said to them, These are the people of the LORD, and are gone forth out of his land. But I had pity for mine holy name....*

God wants His name lifted up and exalted.

> *...which the house of Israel had profaned among the heathen, whither they went. Therefore say unto the house of Israel, Thus saith the Lord GOD; I do not this for your sakes, O house of Israel, but for mine holy name's sake, which ye have profaned among the heathen, whither ye went. And I will sanctify my great name, which was profaned among the heathen, which ye have profaned in the midst of them; and the heathen shall know that I am the LORD, saith the Lord GOD, when I shall be sanctified in you before their eyes* (Ezekiel 36:16-23).

On your job, what do people think of the name of Jesus Christ? Where you live, what do people think of the name of Jesus Christ? What does your family think of the name of the Lord Jesus? At your school, what do people think of the name of the Savior? They can say what they want to about our preaching, our standards, and our Bible. But let them know that Jesus Christ is glorified. This is what is important. Uncompromisingly, let us stand up for God, righteousness, and truth in this God-rejecting, sin-crazed world.

God has a purpose. His purpose is that He be glorified. We put such pressure on ourselves by trying to do God's part. If I lead myself, if I choose my own path, if I walk in the way I want to walk, then I am not glorifying God. This is not God's way.

Why does God allow painful things along our paths, things that are difficult, things that break us, crush us and make us weep? So that as we deal with these circumstances, we will learn to trust Him for the grace to deal with them in such a way that He will be honored and glorified.

It is one thing to deal with life as a Christian; it is another thing to deal with death as a Christian. Is God really who He says He is? Is heaven really what we preach it to be? Is Jesus Christ really able to do what we claim He is able to do? Is He real or is He not real? As we face these challenges, He gives us a blessed opportunity to lift up His name.

You may, at this moment, have an opportunity to lift up His name on the path that He has placed you. You have been given an opportunity to exalt Him and prove He is who He says He is. For His name's sake, we need to trust Him and find the grace we need in every circumstance of life.

The Valley
of the
Shadow of
Death

"Yea, though I walk through the valley of the shadow of death, I will fear no evil: for thou art with me; thy rod and thy staff they comfort me."

Psalm 23:4

When a baby is born, the baby cries and those standing by rejoice. If that child trusts Christ as Savior and lives for God all his life, when it comes time to die he rejoices and all those standing by cry.

"Yea, though I walk through the valley of the shadow of death, I will fear no evil: for thou art with me; thy rod and thy staff they comfort me" (Psalm 23:4).

What does it mean to walk through *"the shadow of death"*? We also find this expression in Psalm 44:19, *"Though thou hast sore broken us in the place of dragons, and covered us with the shadow of death."*

Some think this means there is some sort of darkness we go through when we come to the time of dying. But this is not what God's Word teaches.

> *That which we have seen and heard declare we unto you, that ye also may have fellowship with us: and truly our fellowship is with the Father, and with his Son Jesus Christ. And these things write we unto you, that your joy may be full. This then is the message which we have heard of him, and declare unto you, that God is light, and in him is no darkness at all* (I John 1:3-5).

All of my Christian life I have heard people infer from the Twenty-third Psalm that at the time of dying, we enter into some passage of darkness, *"the valley of the shadow of death."* If there is a shadow, the sun is shining somewhere to cast a shadow. The Bible does not teach that at the time of death, a sudden veil of darkness is going to come over us.

"Shadow" here implies the approaching of something, the nearness of something. It does not imply that we are going to enter into darkness but that death is coming. *"Yea, though I walk through the valley of the shadow of death...."* I have not reached death yet, but I know it is out there. *"Yea, though I walk through the valley of the shadow of death, I will fear no evil: for thou art with me."*

Death is quite a mystery. I remember my friend Dr. Curtis Hutson being diagnosed with cancer. Finally the doctors said, "You're not going to get well." About that time his oldest daughter asked him, "Is there anything I can do for you?" He said, "Don't tell anyone I'm going to get well, you'll lose your credibility." One day I asked Dr. Hutson, "Are you afraid of dying?" He said, with a smile, "I don't know. I've never done it before." Of course, God did give him dying grace.

Death is a mystery but not a time of darkness. Death is a divider. Death divides us from the littleness in life. The thought of death divides us from the things that really hold no meaning. Death separates us from things that should not trouble us. The prospect of death, the thought of leaving here, helps us put things in proper place, to establish the right priorities in life.

The Certainty of Death

The Shepherd's Psalm says, *"Yea, though I walk through the valley of the shadow of death, I will fear no evil: for thou art with me."*

If the Lord Jesus does not come soon, we are all going through the door of death, every one of us. Solomon said in Ecclesiastes 3:1-2, *"To every thing there is a season, and a time to every purpose under the heaven: A time to be born, and a time to die."* Just as surely as there is a time to be born, the Bible says there is a time to die. We cannot escape it.

One day, as I was walking down a hallway in our Christian school in Paterson, New Jersey, I heard a thud in one of the rooms. When I looked inside, I saw the custodian lying on the floor. As I rushed into the room, I found that he was already dead. When the paramedics arrived, they informed me that more than likely he was dead by the time he hit the floor.

> *The thought of death divides us from the things that really hold no meaning.*

Death may come suddenly, or it may come as a result of a lingering illness. Death may come through an accident. No matter how it comes, there is no doubt that death is coming. It is inescapable; we can do nothing to keep it from occurring. Death is going to take place. The Bible says it is *"appointed unto men once to die."*

The Comfort in Death

David says, *"Yea, though I walk through the valley of the shadow of death."* God's children find comfort in the time of death. They find this comfort, not in things, but in a Person. Look again at verses one through four, *"The LORD is my shepherd; I shall not*

102

want. He maketh me to lie down in green pastures: he leadeth me beside the still waters. He restoreth my soul: he leadeth me in the paths of righteousness for his name's sake. Yea, though I walk through the valley of the shadow of death, I will fear no evil: for thou art with me."

Comfort does not come from what we have, what we are, or what we have accomplished in our lives. If you think that you will look back in the fleeting moment of death and think about what you have done, what you are, and what you have owned, you are wrong. There is no comfort in these things. We find comfort only in the Person of Jesus Christ. We are comforted to know He is with us.

In Romans 8 we find a great question in verse thirty-five. The Bible says, *"Who shall separate us from the love of Christ...?"* Then we find a list. Meditate on this list. *"...shall tribulation, or distress, or persecution, or famine, or nakedness, or peril, or sword?"*

Shall tribulation separate us from the love of Christ? Shall distress? Shall persecution? Shall famine and nakedness? After peril, we come to the word *"sword"* which means death by beheading.

The Bible says in verses thirty-six through thirty-nine,

> *As it is written, For thy sake we are killed all the day long; we are accounted as sheep for the slaughter. Nay, in all these things we are more than conquerors through him that loved us. For I am persuaded, that neither death, nor life, nor angels, nor principalities, nor powers, nor things present, nor things to come, Nor height, nor depth, nor any other creature, shall be able to separate us from the love of God, which is in Christ Jesus our Lord.*

Nothing can separate us from the Lord. This is the Shepherd's Psalm. The psalmist speaks of *"the valley of the shadow of death."* He says, "When death is coming upon me, I am not going to fear for Thou art with me."

When God is there, there will be no darkness. There can be no darkness because in Him is no darkness at all. Let us consider another wonderful promise in the book of Hebrews. The Bible says in Hebrews 13:5, *"Let your conversation be without covetousness; and be content with such things as ye have...."* God gives us a great command. Do not covet; be content. We are guilty of breaking this command every day we live. We are guilty because we do covet, and we are not content. We think God has not been good enough to us.

"Be content with such things as ye have...." How do we accomplish this? *"...For he hath said, I will never leave thee, nor forsake thee."* There it is. We have the Lord Jesus. When we have Jesus Christ, we have everything we need.

Every plan and scheme in life comes to an end. Imagine a family sitting in an oncologist's office when the doctor walks in to speak to the family. The children are there with their mother who is ill, waiting for the word from the doctor. Extensive testing has been done. They have imagined that there are tumors in her brain and her lungs, so they will not try anything else.

The doctor comes back and says, "There are no tumors in the brain or in the lungs, but there is an extensive cancerous tumor in the liver." The doctor says, "Here is what we are going to do. We are going to give you chemotherapy directly into the liver to try to reduce this tumor. We are going to fight it."

Can you imagine a family so excited about chemotherapy that they begin weeping, embracing, and rejoicing? Instead of the doctor walking in and saying, "We are going to leave you to die," he says, "We are going to try one more thing." The doctor knows that if he can try one more thing, he keeps holding out hope.

At some point, you weigh the quality and quantity of life. The scales tip one way or the other. You must make decisions about whether the time is going to be what we might call "quality time."

My brother, two sisters and I were in that doctor's office with our mother. We were so excited that we wept and embraced. But then we had to face what would come after the decision to fight it. What then? In that moment when the shadow became substance, at that moment when what was anticipated became reality, what then? At that moment when we walk through that valley like my mother did, what then?

It is not what, but Who. He has promised that He will be with us. He will never leave us, nor will He ever forsake us. He does not forsake us in tribulation. He does not forsake us in persecution. He does not forsake us in distress. He does not forsake us in peril. And He will not forsake us in that moment of death.

For the child of God, death will not be a time of darkness and separation. Instead, death will be the time when we meet the Lord Jesus. We can find such comfort in death in the presence of our wonderful Savior!

The Conqueror of Death

"Yea, though I walk through the valley of the shadow of death...." As the shepherd leads his sheep, the Bible says he leads them *"through"* the valley of the shadow of death. They are not going into the valley to stay there; he is leading them *"through the valley of the shadow of death."*

For the sheep, the valley was a place where water could be found. The valley was a place where the gentle slopes inclining upward led toward higher ground, where better nourishment could be found. But, to get there they must go *"through the valley of the shadow of death."*

The shepherd was not guessing where he should take the sheep next. He was not wondering where he could find good ground. The shepherd had already been there. He knew exactly where he was leading the sheep. He was not trying to find a place to graze. He had already made the journey. He had been there and had come back, and he was going to take the sheep where he had already been.

Our dear Savior, the Lord Jesus, is not guessing about death and dying. He has already been there. He has gone through it, and He is coming back for us to take us where He has already been. He leads us *"through the valley of the shadow of death."*

> *Verily, verily, I say unto you, He that entereth not by the door into the sheepfold, but climbeth up some other way, the same is a thief and a robber. But he that entereth in by the door is the shepherd of the sheep. To him the porter openeth; and the sheep hear his voice: and he calleth his own sheep by name, and leadeth them out. And when he putteth forth his own sheep, he goeth before them* (John 10:1-4).

Notice the expression in verse four, *"He goeth before them."* He does not send them out to some strange place. He says, "I've been there. I will be with you when you are going through it. I know where you are going. I have already done this. I have gone before you."

The Lord Jesus Christ came to earth, was robed in flesh, born in a manger, lived a sinless life, and went to Calvary to pay the sin debt of the whole world. He bore our sins in His own body. He shed His blood. He died for us. He was buried in a borrowed tomb. On the third day, He came forth from the grave, alive forevermore. He said, "I have the keys to death, hell, and the grave."

As a child, God did something for me by allowing my father to be taken early in my life. He used something in the death of my father to help me understand the urgency of life.

My wife's father, who was a Baptist preacher, was killed in an automobile accident when she was only five years old. I believe God used that in her life.

The very subject of death, the thought of death, is a subject pushed back, crowded back somewhere in our minds so as to give as little thought as possible to death until we are forced to think about it. I do not believe this is the way it should be. The thought of death is a motivating thought, such a powerful thought, a thought of such reality that it helps us in our walk with God.

When a child says, "I don't want to die and go to hell," people should not say, "What a terrible thing that he is having those kinds of thoughts." No, it is good to have those thoughts. We are not trying to scare our children, but we want them to understand the reality of death and hell. They do not have to dwell on death forever because they can find hope in Christ and find that He is the Deliverer. He has conquered death, hell, and the grave. They can trust Him.

We may feel young and invincible, but if we do not think about death before getting old, we are going to make some terrible decisions in our lives. Thinking about death when we are young is good. When we are caused to think of death or when someone near us is dying, it is profitable for us. God uses this to bring us to realize the brevity of life and what we should be doing with our lives.

Our nation is laughing her way to hell, but it is not a laughing matter. The lost are separated from God because of their sin, but think about the moment when a man will be separated from God forever.

I understand that *"a merry heart doeth good like a medicine."* I like to laugh, but I am walking among the dead. They are dead in their trespasses and sins and are one breath from eternity. That is an urgent matter.

When the Lord called me to preach, my wife's grandfather said, "Don't let it drive you crazy." What that dear old gentleman meant was, "Don't dwell on it night and day to the point that it drives you down and you are crushed beneath the burden of the sin of the world." I valued that. He gave me sound advice.

We should be like the doctor who always walked into the hospital with a smile on his face, even amid the worst of illnesses. A nurse asked him, "How can you always have a smile?" He answered her, "When I am doing examinations and dealing with my patients, I am not thinking about their illnesses; I am thinking of the cure."

We must think of the cure. The cure is the blood of the Lord Jesus. Do not get the idea that you are going to escape death because you are a Christian. You may ask, "What about the Second Coming of Christ?" He is coming soon. I believe He may come today. I look for His appearing and do my best to enter into communion with Him and actually love the thought of His appearing every day I live.

But what if He does not come soon? We still have hope. Our hope is in the same One. He is coming. Our hope is in the Christ who has conquered death, who has gone before His sheep. Our hope is not in the Second Coming of Christ, but rather in the Christ of the Second Coming.

During my freshman year in college, I met a skeptic. He was from another country. He wanted to be just as outspoken as he possibly could and make a reputation for himself. He would say in his conversations with people, "I don't believe the Bible. I don't believe in heaven. I don't believe in hell." He wanted everyone to know what he believed. I imagine that he thought he was an intellectual.

One day he said to me, "When you die, you will just go into the grave, and that is it. The worms will eat your body." I said to him, "What if someone could die and could come back from the dead and prove differently?" He admitted that it would be interesting to have a conversation with such a person. I tried to explain to him that this is exactly what Jesus Christ did. Whether or not he believed, I do not know.

The Lord Jesus had a similar conversation with Thomas, His disciple.

> *But Thomas, one of the twelve, called Didymus, was not with them when Jesus came. The other disciples therefore said unto him, We have seen the Lord. But he said unto them, Except I shall see in his hands the print of the nails, and put my finger into the print of the nails, and thrust my hand into his side, I will not believe. And after eight days again his disciples were within, and Thomas with them: then came Jesus, the doors being shut, and stood in the midst, and said, Peace be unto you. Then saith he to Thomas, Reach hither thy finger, and behold my hands; and reach hither thy hand, and thrust it into my side: and be not faithless, but believing. And Thomas answered and said unto him, My Lord and my God. Jesus saith unto him, Thomas, because thou hast seen me, thou hast believed: blessed are they that have not seen, and yet have believed* (John 20:24-29).

Our hope is not in the Second Coming of Christ, but rather in the Christ of the Second Coming.

If only we could read this passage the same way the Lord Jesus spoke to Thomas. The Lord Jesus tenderly spoke to Thomas when He appeared to him. When Thomas heard the Lord Jesus, he did not have to touch His hands and side. He simply cried out, *"My Lord and my*

God." John wrote in verse twenty-nine, *"Jesus saith unto him, Thomas, because thou hast seen me, thou hast believed: blessed are they that have not seen, and yet have believed."*

I want to write my name at the end of verse twenty-nine. I did not see Him. I have yet to see His hands and His side. But I want you to know something–I believe. I believe He conquered death, hell, and the grave. You can choose to believe what you wish, but I believe Him.

Death is certain, but I will have comfort in that moment because my Shepherd will be with me. Not only will He be with me, but He has also conquered death, hell, and the grave, and all will be well. I will not be alone, no matter what the circumstances may be. He has promised, *"I will never leave thee, nor forsake thee."*

Thy Rod and Thy Staff

"Yea, though I walk through the valley of the shadow of death, I will fear no evil: for thou art with me; thy rod and thy staff they comfort me."

Psalm 23:4

---

iving in perilous times makes comfort difficult to find; however, as sheep we find comfort in the presence of the Shepherd. As we move deeper into the Twenty-third Psalm, we move closer and closer to the Shepherd.

Our Shepherd Is Personal

The Bible says in Psalm 23:4, *"Yea, though I walk through the valley of the shadow of death, I will fear no evil: for thou art with me."* The psalmist is no longer speaking *about* the Shepherd; he is speaking *to* the Shepherd. He is no longer saying about the Shepherd, He *"is my shepherd...He maketh me to lie down in green pastures...He leadeth me beside the still waters...He restoreth my soul...He leadeth me in the paths of righteousness for his name's sake."* He is no longer speaking from a distance. He is now in communion with Him.

Verse four says, *"Yea, though I walk through the valley of the shadow of death, I will fear no evil: for thou art with me."* Here David is speaking *to* the Lord.

Our Shepherd is personal. It is much easier to talk about the Lord than to talk with Him. We say things such as, "I have a wonderful Savior. He is a great Savior. He provides all my needs." We are bragging on Him, and we should be. We should be exalting Him by

114

testifying about Him. However, there is a world of difference between talking *about* Him and talking *to* Him, communing with Him.

In Job 1:1, the account begins, *"There was a man in the land of Uz, whose name was Job; and that man was perfect and upright, and one that feared God, and eschewed evil."* In the eyes of the Lord, Job was a great man. The Lord said that he was upright and perfect and that he feared God and eschewed evil.

I am sure that Job could talk about the Lord just as we can. But after God dealt with Job and purged his life, we read,

> Then Job answered the LORD, and said, I know that thou canst do every thing, and that no thought can be withholden from thee. Who is he that hideth counsel without knowledge? therefore have I uttered that I understood not; things too wonderful for me, which I knew not.

Job said, "When I spoke, I really did not understand what I was saying."

> Hear, I beseech thee, and I will speak: I will demand of thee, and declare thou unto me. I have heard of thee by the hearing of the ear: but now mine eye seeth thee. Wherefore I abhor myself, and repent in dust and ashes (Job 42:1-6).

Job said, "Lord, now I know You, not just about You. I can give this testimony: it is as though I had only heard of You before, but now I know You."

I wonder how many of us are willing to admit that we are at the place in our Christian lives where we simply talk about the Lord, brag about the Lord, tell people about the Lord, but we do not have much personal communion with the Lord Jesus.

A young man said to me recently that he was considering how desperately he needed to spend time in prayer and communion with

God and time in prayer and fasting. The subject of serving the Lord and doing things for God was being discussed. In the conversation, the statement was made that we place such emphasis on serving, soul winning, and witnessing–and we should. We place such emphasis on telling people about the Lord–and we should. We place such emphasis on doing something for God–and we should after all He has done for us. But, you and I both know we have not placed the right emphasis on communing with God, spending time with God, praying and fasting, being alone with God, and coming to know God as we should know Him.

Our Shepherd is personal. We are not to view Him from a distance; we are to commune with Him.

We love reading, *"The LORD is my shepherd; I shall not want."* We love, *"He leadeth me."* We love it all. *"He restoreth my soul."* It is all beautiful. But can you see the progression here? It is deeper and deeper into the heart of God.

Finally, as the sheep walks *"through the valley of the shadow of death,"* he says, *"Thou art with me."* We are not going to make it victoriously through the great trials of life until we learn this truth–our God is personal, and He is with us.

He cannot be simply a fact that we quote. Oh, we know He said He will never leave us or forsake us, but He must be a reality in our daily lives. We must have faith in God and know *"thou art with me."*

Consider the testimony of the apostle Paul. Many years after he was saved on the road to Damascus, many years after he gave his life to serve the Lord, he wrote the church in Philippi,

> *Finally, my brethren, rejoice in the Lord. To write the same things to you, to me indeed is not grievous, but for you it is safe. Beware of dogs, beware of evil workers, beware of the concision. For we are the circumcision, which worship God in the spirit, and rejoice in Christ Jesus, and have no confidence in the*

116

flesh. Though I might also have confidence in the flesh. If any other man thinketh that he hath whereof he might trust in the flesh, I more: Circumcised the eighth day, of the stock of Israel, of the tribe of Benjamin, an Hebrew of the Hebrews; as touching the law, a P h a r i s e e ; Concerning zeal, persecuting the church; touching the righteousness which is in the law, blameless. But what things were gain to me, those I counted loss for Christ. Yea doubtless, and I count all things but loss for the excellency of the knowledge of Christ Jesus my Lord: for whom I have suffered the loss of all things, and do count them but dung, that I may win Christ.

> *We are not going to make it, not victoriously, through the great trials of life until we learn this truth–our God is personal, and He is with us.*

Paul said, "Everything I had, everything I was, everything I claim to be, compared to Jesus Christ, is like the dung of a barnyard."

And be found in him, not having mine own righteousness, which is of the law, but that which is through the faith of Christ, the righteousness which is of God by faith: That I may know him (Philippians 3:1-10).

Paul said, "Yes, I serve Him. Yes, I live for Him. Yes, I preach about Him. Yes, I testify of Him. However, all of this is not in order to know Him, but because I know Him I speak of Him, serve Him, and do for Him."

Our Shepherd is personal. He is not a god somewhere on a pole or displayed somewhere for us to see. He is the God who lives in us. Our Shepherd is personal. I am moved as I read the words of this beautiful psalm, *"Thou art with me."* David is not talking *about* Him, but talking *to* Him. May God move upon our hearts to bring us into this kind of communion with Christ.

What will it take for Him to really break through in our lives? I am a part of a strong church, a Bible-believing, Bible-preaching church. I would not be in any other kind of church. We gather information about the Bible and the things of God and about what we should be doing and what we should be saying. But, what will it take for the Lord to break through all the facts, the figures, and the ideas? What will it take for us to cleave to Him, to lean on Him, to walk with Him, to commune with Him, to know Him, and to fellowship with Him?

The Lord does not want a distant glance from us; He wants a close, personal relationship with us.

This is illustrated well in our homes. Ladies, you can be married to a man and know what time he goes to work and what time he is expected to come home. You can know where he works and what he does at his job. You can know what he likes to eat and what he likes to do. You can know everything about him but at times feel as if you are living in the house with someone who is just a "fact" and you have no real, intimate fellowship with your husband.

God does not want that kind of relationship with His children. He does not want a distant glance from us; He wants a close, personal relationship with us. Our Shepherd is personal.

Our Shepherd Is Powerful

The Bible says in Psalm 23:4, *"Thy rod and thy staff they comfort me."* The shepherd uses simple things. He used a rod and a staff. The rod was a weapon. It was not a gun, a bow and arrow, or a spear. It was a stick, a club-like thing, a rod. The rod was used to guard the sheep.

Young people who were growing up and working as shepherds learned how to use that rod. They could learn to throw it with great accuracy at long distances. They could hit their target well with the rod. It became an extension of their bodies.

The shepherds also carried a staff. The staff was a long stick, longer than the rod and most often with a curved end. The staff was used to lean on, of course. However, the staff was used in particular to guide the sheep or to retrieve the sheep. If a lamb happened to be wandering away, the shepherd could reach out with the staff and with the crooked end bring the sheep back.

If a little lamb fell into the water and was in danger, the shepherd could reach with that staff and hook it around the body of the little lamb and bring him up out of the water. If a lamb was entangled somewhere in the briars or was caught in a thicket and could not get out, the staff could be used to tear loose the things that had gotten tangled in his wool and free him.

When the sheep observed that the shepherd had the rod to guard and the staff to guide, he was comforted. The sheep realized that the shepherd had all the power he needed and said, *"Thy rod and thy staff they comfort me."*

Let us look at a few things from other passages in the Bible about this rod and staff. Moses had been given the responsibility of leading the children of Israel out of Egyptian bondage. He led them out, and they came to the Red Sea. The sea was in front of them, and the armies of Pharaoh were behind them. Of course, they started complaining.

> *And when Pharaoh drew nigh, the children of Israel lifted up their eyes, and, behold, the Egyptians marched after them; and they were sore afraid: and the children of Israel cried out unto the LORD. And they said unto Moses, Because there were no graves in Egypt, hast thou taken us away to die in the wilderness? wherefore hast thou dealt thus with us, to carry us forth out of Egypt? Is not this the word that we did tell thee in Egypt, saying, Let us alone, that we may serve the Egyptians? For it had been better for us to serve the Egyptians, than that we should die in the wilderness* (Exodus 14:10-12).

They said, "Moses, you've brought us out here to die in the wilderness. We would rather be in Egypt and die there."

The Bible says in Exodus 14:13, *"And Moses said unto the people, Fear ye not...."*

The Israelites thought, "The Red Sea is in front of us, and the army of Pharaoh is behind us. We are trapped."

Moses said, *"...Fear ye not, stand still, and see the salvation of the LORD...."*

We are reading from one perspective; they were listening from another. We know how the story ended. We know God opened the sea and they walked through on dry ground. Pharaoh's army went into the sea, and God closed it up. But Moses said,

> *Fear ye not, stand still, and see the salvation of the LORD, which he will show to you to day: for the Egyptians whom ye have seen to day, ye shall see them again no more for ever. The LORD shall fight for you, and ye shall hold your peace.*

I like to fight for myself, and you do too. As a matter of fact, this is part of our old nature. All of us have besetting sins. I have dealt with my temper all my life. Temper is like a current in the river: you need a little of it to keep the water moving. However, if you get too much of it, it becomes very dangerous.

Anger is not a terribly bad thing. If controlled, it can be used the right way. If it is out of control, it can be awful. We can kill with our words. We want to fight. We want to act. But God said, *"Stand still."* The Lord said, *"The LORD shall fight for you, and ye shall hold your peace."* May the Lord help us to do this!

The story continues in verse fifteen, *"And the LORD said unto Moses, Wherefore criest thou unto me? speak unto the children of Israel, that they go forward: But lift thou up thy rod...."* Here we see *"the rod."* This is the same kind of rod mentioned in Psalm 23. Do you remember all the things God did with Moses' rod?

He said, *"But lift thou up thy rod,"* that symbol of power, that symbol of authority.

> *But lift thou up thy rod, and stretch out thine hand over the sea, and divide it: and the children of Israel shall go on dry ground through the midst of the sea. And I, behold, I will harden the hearts of the Egyptians, and they shall follow them: and I will get me honour upon Pharaoh, and upon all his host, upon his chariots, and upon his horsemen. And the Egyptians shall know that I am the LORD, when I have gotten me honour upon Pharaoh, upon his chariots, and upon his horsemen (Exodus 14:16-18).*

God said, "Stretch out that rod," and Moses did.

When a Hebrew who knew his Bible read Psalm 23 and came to the expression of that rod, that powerful rod, he would think about what God is able to do to deliver His own and to defeat His enemies.

In Leviticus 27:32 the Bible says, *"And concerning the tithe of the herd, or of the flock, even of whatsoever passeth under the rod, the tenth shall be holy unto the LORD."*

A shepherd would use his rod, the same rod that he used to guard, as a weapon to defend the sheep, to protect the sheep. He also used this rod to count the sheep. The sheep would pass under the rod and be counted.

The same hand that deals with us and chastens us is the hand that cares for us and loves us. We know this from rearing our own children, do we not? We tell them, "You cannot do that, and you will be punished if you do." Our children are punished and disciplined when they do wrong. But, we punish and discipline with the same hand that loves and embraces them. God does the same for us.

The shepherd would take the rod and count his sheep as they passed under the rod. He would actually touch them with the rod. They knew something of his care from his rod. They saw that same rod being used on their adversaries. They passed under the rod, and he touched them with that same rod, counting them and calling them by name. At the same time, the shepherd would part their wool with that rod to look beneath the surface and see if anything harmful had happened to them during the day.

As the shepherd parted the wool of the sheep and searched their little bodies beneath the surface with that rod, he might find a wound where oil needed to be applied. He might find some disease on their flesh. He might notice something that would eventually take the life of that lamb if not cared for properly. He would part the wool with that rod and look beneath the surface.

That is what the psalmist is talking about in Psalm 139:23-24, *"Search me, O God, and know my heart: try me, and know my thoughts: And see if there be any wicked way in me, and lead me in the way everlasting."*

The word *"search"* means "to look beneath the surface." As the sheep passed under the rod, the shepherd looked beneath the surface of their wool. He looked down into the wool, down on the flesh. The psalmist prayed in Psalm 139:23, "Search me, Lord. Look beneath the surface of my life. Show me, Lord, what I need. Find in me what should not be in me." This is the way the rod was used.

I praise God for the things He has stopped in my life. Most of us talk about what God has started. Have you ever thanked God for what He has stopped? He may have stopped where you were headed, what you were going to do, who you were going to be with that you should not have been with, or things you were going to do that you should not have done. God stopped you. Perhaps it involved things you were going to achieve for yourself or purchase for yourself, and you can thank God now you never got involved. Oh, how I thank Him that He puts us under the rod and searches us.

The same hand that deals with us and chastens us is the hand that cares for us and loves us.

The shepherd used the staff to guide the sheep if they got out of line. I am told that a shepherd could walk by a sheep that had become

123

jittery and nervous and by simply laying that staff against the body of the sheep, the sheep would walk along side the shepherd. The sheep would be comforted and calmed by the staff of the shepherd simply lying against his body as he walked. The shepherd used the staff to guide his sheep.

The rod represents to us the powerful Word of God, and the staff represents the Spirit of God that God has given to guide us. The psalmist comes to *"the valley of the shadow of death,"* and he says, "My Shepherd is personal; He is here with me. My Shepherd is powerful. He has a rod. He has a staff. I have nothing to fear. Whatever enemy I may face, He will use a rod on him. If I cannot find my way, He will show me the way with His staff. His rod and staff comfort me."

Our Shepherd Is Present

Our Shepherd is not only personal and powerful, but He is always present. Someone is near you. He is present; He is here. He wants us to remember that He is the Shepherd who is present with us.

When you get into something you should not be involved in as one of His children, you do not have to say, "I must find the Lord. He is out yonder somewhere. I don't know where He is, but I'm going to have to find God." No, the Lord is with you. He is present with you.

The most sobering thing about being in the place of worship is that we enter into the presence of God. He is here. Think how important it is that we can call on the Lord, and He is present.

Let us go back to our story about Moses leading the children of Israel out of Egyptian bondage. Consider again Exodus 3. Moses was eighty years old, out in the desert, and God called him. He spoke to him through a burning bush. The bush was burning, yet it was not consumed. This is the first beautiful picture of the nation of Israel, persecuted but never consumed.

God spoke to Moses through that burning bush. He said, "Moses, I want you to go down and tell Pharaoh to let My people go."

Moses had grown up in the household of Pharaoh. He had seen the might and power of Egypt. He realized that he had to have more power than Pharaoh, and Pharaoh was very powerful. Only God could give him this special anointing.

> *And Moses said unto God, Behold, when I come unto the children of Israel, and shall say unto them, The God of your fathers hath sent me unto you; and they shall say to me, What is his name? what shall I say unto them? And God said unto Moses, I AM THAT I AM* (Exodus 3:13-14).

He did not say, "I was" or "I will be," but He said "*I AM THAT I AM.*" God said, *"I AM,"* not "used to be," or "going to be," but He said *"I AM."*

We have a past. For most, it is not very pretty. We have a future that can be extremely fearful. God has given us forgiveness for the past and faith for the future.

God has no past and no future. We have a past with God and a future with God. But God is not a God of past and future things. He is a God always present. He is eternally existent. He has no beginning; He has no ending; He has no middle. He has no marking place to say everything here is past, everything here is future. He is always the same. He says, *"I AM."*

What does this mean for us? It means that whatever we are facing in life, whatever we have to deal with in life, whenever we have to deal with it, God is always present. He is here.

The Lord Jesus once said to the Jews that had gathered against Him,

> *Your father Abraham rejoiced to see my day: and he saw it, and was glad. Then said the Jews unto him, Thou art not yet fifty years old, and hast thou seen Abraham?* (John 8:56-57).

They said, "Abraham lived centuries ago. You are not even fifty. How can You say before Abraham was, You existed?"

The Lord Jesus answered them in verse fifty-eight, *"Verily, verily, I say unto you, Before Abraham was, I AM."*

Do you ever think about God and who God really is? I am sure that you do. Remember this: God always is. Some people get the idea that the Lord is weak and feeble and unable to cope with the great problems of our day. As Christians, we should not think this way.

Our God is the God of the present. He is always present. He is the Great *"I AM,"* and He can help you with any need you have this moment. He is greater than anything you face in life. Trust Him now!

In the
Presence of
Mine
Enemies

"Thou preparest a table before me in the presence of mine enemies: thou anointest my head with oil; my cup runneth over."

Psalm 23:5

Our God delights in preparing a table for us in the presence of our enemies. The psalmist says in verse five of Psalm 23, *"Thou preparest a table before me in the presence of mine enemies: thou anointest my head with oil; my cup runneth over."*

As we believe, by faith, the first verse of this psalm, we can take everything in Scripture by faith. The Bible says, *"The Lord is my shepherd."* This verse is like the very first verse in the Bible, Genesis 1:1, *"In the beginning God created the heaven and the earth."* If we take this verse by faith, we will not have trouble with anything else in the Bible.

As we appropriate by faith this first verse of Psalm 23, *"The Lord is my shepherd..."* then we can say, *"...I shall not want."*

There is a powerful story of two dedicated Christian girls who trusted this psalm during their martyrdom. In 1681 two Scottish girls, about twenty years of age, would not yield to the teachings of the Catholic church because of their faith in Christ. Because they rejected the lies of the Roman Catholic church, they paid with their lives.

The bishop, putting them to death in Edinburgh, Scotland, said, "You girls would never listen to the Roman priest, but now you will have to as we put you to death."

The girls' names were Isabelle and Marion. One said to the other, "We don't have to listen now either. Let's sing a song." The other replied, "Yes, the Twenty-third Psalm." As they sang the Twenty-third Psalm, they drowned out the voice of the priest trying to speak to them before their execution. They went out to meet God singing, *"The LORD is my shepherd; I shall not want."* These girls were two faithful Christians who stayed true to the Lord until they saw His face.

Praise the Lord for who He is and for the power of His Word to work in our lives. As we read this expression, *"Thou preparest a table before me in the presence of mine enemies,"* we remember that shepherding was a dangerous work.

Many things could endanger the sheep. Let us consider the testimony David gave to Saul. In I Samuel 17, the giant Goliath came up, making his speech, blaspheming God and the armies of Israel. Many times we refer to this story as the story of David and Goliath, but in reality it is the story of how God used David to defeat Goliath, not simply the story of David and Goliath.

> *And when the words were heard which David spake, they rehearsed them before Saul: and he sent for him. And David said to Saul, Let no man's heart fail because of him; thy servant will go and fight with this Philistine* (I Samuel 17:31-32).

Remember when David came down? Did it just so happen that the giant was making one of his speeches? No. It was divine providence that caused David to hear what the giant said, and David's heart was stirred to do something about it. God needs people who can be stirred to serve Him. I want to be one of them. Do you?

When David came upon the scene and the giant was making his speech, he said,

> *What shall be done to the man that killeth this Philistine, and taketh away the reproach from Israel?*

131

> *for who is this uncircumcised Philistine, that he should defy the armies of the living God? And the people answered him after this manner, saying, So shall it be done to the man that killeth him. And Eliab his eldest brother heard when he spake unto the men; and Eliab's anger was kindled against David, and he said, Why camest thou down hither? and with whom hast thou left those few sheep in the wilderness? I know thy pride, and the naughtiness of thine heart; for thou art come down that thou mightest see the battle. And David said, What have I now done? Is there not a cause?* (I Samuel 17:26-29).

Word went out that David would fight the giant. The Bible tells us in verse thirty-three, *"And Saul said to David, Thou art not able to go against this Philistine to fight with him for thou art but a youth, and he a man of war from his youth."* This is what the world will always be saying. Saul was not talking about how we need God. He was making reference to how much we really need to find some human instrument who can match flesh against flesh. This is a temptation we all face.

> *Thy servant kept his father's sheep, and there came a lion, and a bear, and took a lamb out of the flock: and I went out after him, and smote him, and delivered it out of his mouth: and when he arose against me, I caught him by his beard, and smote him, and slew him. Thy servant slew both the lion and the bear: and this uncircumcised Philistine shall be as one of them, seeing he hath defied the armies of the living God* (I Samuel 17:34-36).

Of course, the story ends with God proving Himself through David. Just as David prayed, all the earth knew there was a God in Israel because of the victory that God gave to David.

The point is that David was a shepherd. He said to Saul, "I am going to tell you about shepherding. It can be dangerous business. There are enemies out there. I have done hand-to-hand combat with a lion and a bear."

Most of us, when we think about a lion and a bear, imagine looking at one from a distance. But David said, "I had my hands in his fur. I took my lamb out of his mouth. I looked him eye to eye." The enemy is out there. Shepherding is a dangerous duty. Poisonous plants can take the lives of little lambs. Bad water can destroy their health and bring about their death. Wild creatures can ravage them.

As God gave David the words of Psalm 23 to pen, when he came to this expression, *"Thou preparest a table before me in the presence of mine enemies,"* no doubt his mind flashed with potential enemies. He thought of his own enemies: how Saul tried to take his life, how his own children rebelled against him, and how his followers spoke of stoning him that day in Ziklag. God had delivered him.

The Preparation of the Table

The Bible says, *"Thou preparest a table."* It is not the sheep's responsibility to feed himself. He is brought to a certain place to graze, but it is the shepherd's responsibility to find the food or the grazing area for the sheep.

All of us are apt to take too much upon ourselves. We find it difficult to discern between the divine and the human. What are we to do, and what do we allow God to do through us?

The psalmist says, *"Thou preparest a table before me."* The word *"table"* could mean flat table areas where the sheep could graze easily. We know that it also means a table spread with food upon it or a grazing area where the sheep could receive nourishment.

The sheep is speaking here of the Shepherd, *"Thou preparest a table before me."* God does the preparing; He does the blessing. What do we need? God is able to care for whatever we need in our lives. The Bible says in Philippians 4:19, *"But my God shall supply all your need according to his riches in glory by Christ Jesus."* We cannot name a need that God cannot provide. God's Word says in Ephesians 3:20 that He is able to do *"exceeding abundantly above all that we ask or think."* Our God can do all things. He is able to prepare a table before us in the presence of our enemies.

In Psalm 78, one of the historical psalms, the Lord talks about His people and their lack of faith. In verses eighteen through nineteen, the Bible says, *"And they tempted God in their heart by asking meat for their lust. Yea, they spake against God; they said, Can God furnish a table in the wilderness?"*

Any time we ask if God can, we have asked the wrong question. Dr. Harold Sightler, who is now walking the streets of gold and looking into the face of Jesus Christ, preached a great message on *"Can God?"* In his message he answered the question, "God can! God can!"

They said, *"Can God?"*

> *Behold, he smote the rock, that the waters gushed out, and the streams overflowed; can he give bread also? can he provide flesh for his people? Therefore the LORD heard this, and was wroth: so a fire was kindled against Jacob, and anger also came up against Israel; because they believed not in God, and trusted not in his salvation: though he had commanded the clouds from above, and opened the doors of heaven, and had rained down manna upon them to eat, and had given them of the corn of heaven. Man did eat angels' food: he sent them meat to the full. He caused an east wind to blow in the heaven: and by his power he brought in the south*

134

wind. He rained flesh also upon them as dust, and feathered fowls like as the sand of the sea: and he let it fall in the midst of their camp, round about their habitations. So they did eat, and were well filled: for he gave them their own desire; they were not estranged from their lust. But while their meat was yet in their mouths, the wrath of God came upon them, and slew the fattest of them, and smote down the chosen men of Israel. For all this they sinned still, and believed not for his wondrous works. Therefore their days did he consume in vanity, and their years in trouble. When he slew them, then they sought him: and they returned and inquired early after God (Psalm 78:20-34).

We think, "When will this nation of ours seek the Lord? What must happen to our beloved nation before we turn to God?" God said in II Chronicles 7:14,

If my people, which are called by my name, shall humble themselves, and pray, and seek my face, and turn from their wicked ways; then will I hear from heaven, and will forgive their sin, and will heal their land.

God has no problem with being able to hear from heaven. He has no problem forgiving our sin and healing our land. He is abundantly able to do it. As His people, we have a problem calling on His name, humbling ourselves and turning from our wicked ways. He did not say if folks in the nation's capitol do this; He did say if folks in the church house would do this, then He would hear us, forgive us, and heal our land.

And they remembered that God was their rock, and the high God their redeemer. Nevertheless they did flatter him with their mouth, and they lied unto him with their tongues. For their heart was not right with him,

135

> *neither were they stedfast in his covenant. But he, being full of compassion, forgave their iniquity, and destroyed them not: yea, many a time turned he his anger away, and did not stir up all his wrath. For he remembered that they were but flesh; a wind that passeth away, and cometh not again. How oft did they provoke him in the wilderness, and grieve him in the desert! Yea, they turned back and tempted God, and limited the Holy One of Israel* (Psalm 78:35-41).

The Bible says that God *"remembered that they were but flesh; a wind that passeth away, and cometh not again."*

I have lived to see many breezy days when the wind crossed my face and moved on. I am praying that the next time the wind brushes against your cheeks it will cause you to remember this passage from Psalm 78 and that you will remember that God said this is how brief our lives are–as a wind that blows and never comes again.

How can a life that is just a short breeze amount to anything? How can we invest our lives, this short span we have that God compares to the wind? We can only do this one way. We can give it to the eternal God. We can invest it in eternity by serving Jesus Christ–knowing Him, living for Him, loving Him, and serving Him.

In this psalm, the Bible says they *"limited God"*–the God who prepared a table in the wilderness, the God who prepares a table *"in the presence of mine enemies."* How? They limited Him by their unbelief.

The needs are so great, but God is greater! We need the faith to believe God will provide all we need. We need to know the God who can prepare a table for us in the presence of our enemies.

In Romans 8:28-32 the Bible says,

> *And we know that all things work together for good to them that love God, to them who are the called according to his purpose. For whom he did*

foreknow, he also did predestinate to be conformed to the image of his Son, that he might be the firstborn among many brethren. Moreover whom he did predestinate, them he also called: and whom he called, them he also justified: and whom he justified, them he also glorified. What shall we then say to these things? If God be for us, who can be against us? He that spared not his own Son, but delivered him up for us all, how shall he not with him also freely give us all things?

Our silver and our gold do not impress God; our faith is what impresses Him. We limit the Holy One of Israel just as they did in Psalm 78. Just as those people in the wilderness limited God, we limit God when we do not believe Him for what He has for us. The only way to glorify God is to place our faith in Him.

We must believe God and trust Him in the conflict. The real victories are not won sitting outside watching; the real victories are won inside the arena. We must get in the fight.

The psalmist said, *"Thou preparest a table before me."* I need not worry or fret. I do not have to be anxious for anything. My God, my Shepherd, my great God, the God of the universe, the Creator God, has prepared a table before me.

Do you know what it took to prepare that table? It took Calvary. God's Son came to earth and bled and died for our sins. He paid the awful price that must be paid. The billows of God's wrath rolled over the Lord Jesus. God's Word says in II Corinthians 5:21, *"For he hath made him to be sin for us, who knew no sin; that we might be made the righteousness of God in him."* He conquered every foe. He arose victoriously from the grave, alive forevermore. We have a risen Savior. We have an ascended Savior. We have a Mediator sitting at the right hand of God the Father, ever living to make intercession for us. He has prepared a table that provides all our needs. We dine at His table only by faith.

When I come to His table, I can be seated only as I am willing to sit down and rest in Him. What makes me trust Him? What encourages me to come to Him? The second part of Psalm 23:5 says, *"in the presence of mine enemies."* We want to participate in the partaking of the table without the presence of the enemies. However, the presence of enemies causes the sheep to stay close to the Shepherd.

The Presence of the Enemies

"Thou preparest a table before me in the presence of mine enemies." The enemies are real. We face the enemies of the world, the flesh, and the Devil. God uses these enemies as tools to cause us to trust Him, to believe Him, and to receive Him.

The Bible says in John 14:14, *"I have given them thy word; and the world hath hated them, because they are not of the world, even as I am not of the world."* Certain truths in the Bible cause us to pray, "Lord, drive this truth deep into my heart." This is one of those truths, *"they are not of the world, even as I am not of the world."* Many of us live as if this world were our final home.

The Bible continues in verses fifteen through seventeen,

> *I pray not that thou shouldest take them out of the world, but that thou shouldest keep them from the evil. They are not of the world, even as I am not of the world. Sanctify them through thy truth: thy word is truth.*

Our God leaves us in the presence of our enemies. This works for our good because in the presence of our enemies, we recognize our need for the Lord. This works for our good because what we are doing is God's work in the presence of our enemies, telling them about the Lord.

We want all the enemies removed. We want smooth sailing. Let us join with Moses and tell God in the wilderness, "What I would like for You to do, Lord, is remove the Pharaoh. If You can just remove the Pharaoh, I will go back to Egypt."

God says, "I am not going to remove the Pharaoh, but I am going with you to face him. You are going to be standing in the presence of your enemies, but I am going to be standing with you."

Let us go to Babylon with Shadrach, Meshach, and Abednego. Will God remove all the peril? No! God said, "You're going into a fiery furnace, but I am going there with you."

Consider Daniel in the den of lions. God said to him, "Daniel, they are going to cast you into a den of lions, but I am going with you." These two things go hand in hand.

Why do we not trust God for the things we should? Why do we not sit down at God's table, dine by faith, and receive from God's good hand all that He has for us? Why do we have such weak, anemic Christianity? One day when we get to heaven, the Lord will say, "There was so much food on the table that you didn't eat." We fail to see that in the presence of our enemies we are driven to God's table to take from the Lord what we must have to live.

The world is full of enemies, but this world is not our home. There is conflict all around us. When

> *We want to participate in the partaking of the table without the presence of the enemies. However, the presence of enemies causes the sheep to stay close to the Shepherd.*

Paul wrote the church in Philippi in Philippians chapter three, beginning with verse seventeen, the Bible says, *"Brethren, be followers together of me, and mark them which walk so as ye have us for an ensample. (For many walk, of whom I have told you often, and now tell you even weeping...."* This is what we need. We need a generation of weeping Christians who will lift up the truth in love.

Have you come to realize that without a revival we have no hope in this land or anywhere else in this world? We have no options. Our plans, our schemes, our ideas, and our campaigns are absolutely to no avail. We need revival!

When real revival comes, when the real wind of the Holy Spirit blows, people will not only do what they should do; they will have a desire to do what they should be doing.

Paul says in Philippians 3:18, *"I have told you often, and now tell you even weeping, that they are the enemies of the cross."* Paul was in the conflict; he was in the battle. He was in the presence of the enemies. Just as real as David had the fur of a lion in his hands and the eyes of a bear staring him in the face, Paul said, "I am in that kind of conflict. I am in the midst of those kinds of enemies of the cross. If I did not have God to sustain me, to feed me, and to prepare me, I could not make it in the presence of these enemies of the cross."

What we want is smooth sailing, easy living, no bend in the road, no rough places.

> *When real revival comes, when the real wind of the Holy Spirit blows, people will not only do what they should do; they will have a desire to do what they should be doing.*

What do we expect to get with this meandering life we live, taking the road of least resistance, seeking a way where there is no conflict, flinching and dodging everything that even resembles the reproach of the cross? What kind of life do we hope to have? What we get is a weak, anemic life that does not call on an Almighty God to provide the table that He is able to provide. We come to the table because of the enemies.

In I John 4:4, the Bible says, *"Ye are of God, little children, and have overcome them: because greater is he that is in you, than he that is in the world."*

A lion is somewhere out there on the horizon. The shepherd can see the sheep talking to one another. One little lamb says to the other, "There is a lion, there is a bear out there." And someone among the flock says, "Don't worry about the lion and the bear. Keep your eyes on the shepherd. He'll take care of the lion and the bear."

One might say to the other, "I don't know if I am supposed to eat this." A wise sheep would say, "Don't worry about it. The shepherd would not have brought us to this table to feed us anything that was not good for us."

Stay close to Him. Lean on Him. If we could take our lives and divide them into periods of time, like marks on a ruler, we could see segments of our lives when we really trusted God and God was real. In that segment when we trusted God, we would also see something we had to face that drove us to the Lord.

If you say, "There was a time when I came by faith and really rested and dined at the table the Lord prepared for me," you would also see that when you were at that table, you were in the presence of enemies. You had sought the Lord's table. *"Thou preparest a table before me in the presence of mine enemies."*

As I read this verse in I John 4:4, *"Ye are of God, little children, and have overcome them: because greater is he that is in you, than he that is in the world,"* the Holy Spirit reminds me that we are not working *for* victory, but we are working *from* victory. We are working from the victory Christ has already won on Calvary through His death, burial, and resurrection. He has proven that He is victorious. Nothing we are facing should destroy us *"because greater is he that is in you, than he that is in the world."* We are working from His victory. In Romans 8:37, God's Word says, *"We are more than conquerors through Him that loved us."*

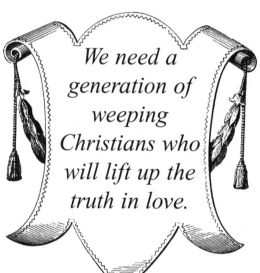

We need a generation of weeping Christians who will lift up the truth in love.

When we are out grazing and we are hungry, the Shepherd will lead us to the tablelands. On the tablelands, He will have the table spread.

You may say, "What about the enemies?" Do not worry about the enemies. Just keep looking at the Shepherd because He will prepare a table before us in the presence of our enemies. We are in the world, but not of the world.

God delights to prove Himself in the presence of our enemies. He smiles because His children do not simply squeeze through–they march through in victory in the presence of the enemies. This is the kind of table God prepares for His children.

By faith, let us claim what God has for us. Do not count the foes; do not count the enemies. In the presence of our enemies, God prepares a table for us.

Take from the table what you need. Appropriate by faith what you need this day for what is troubling you, for what is worrying you, and for what is frightening you. Take from this table what you need. If He has given us His Son, as the Bible says in Romans 8:32, we know that He will *"freely give us all things."*

My Cup Runneth Over

"Thou preparest a table before me in the presence of mine enemies: thou anointest my head with oil; my cup runneth over."

Psalm 23:5

---

iving in the overflow is the Lord's design for each of His children. How many Christians are living in spiritual poverty?

The psalmist says in Psalm 23:5, *"Thou preparest a table before me in the presence of mine enemies: thou anointest my head with oil; my cup runneth over."* This anointing of the head is a beautiful picture of love, courtesy, and kindness. We see it expressed to our Savior in Matthew 26:6-12,

> *Now when Jesus was in Bethany, in the house of Simon the leper, there came unto him a woman having an alabaster box of very precious ointment, and poured it on his head, as he sat at meat.*

As Christ entered the house, His head was anointed with oil.

> *But when his disciples saw it, they had indignation, saying, To what purpose is this waste? For this ointment might have been sold for much, and given to the poor. When Jesus understood it, he said unto them, Why trouble ye the woman? for she hath wrought a good work upon me. For ye have the poor always with you; but me ye have not always. For in that she hath poured this ointment on my body, she did it for my burial.*

This woman who anointed the Lord Jesus had a discerning spirit. She understood that Christ was going to bleed and die for the sins of the whole world. God led her in this. When Christ entered the house, she anointed His head with oil, filling the room with a beautiful fragrance. The fragrance would linger and would be long remembered. This was an act of her kindness and love.

Thinking about how this took place as Christ entered the house, consider with me again Psalm 23:6. We are about to enter the house of the Lord. *"Surely goodness and mercy shall follow me all the days of my life: and I will dwell in the house of the LORD for ever."*

We should go into heaven with the wonderful fragrance of Jesus Christ. We should enter into God's house to dwell forever with His holy anointing upon us.

The Oil

As we consider the oil of this anointing, we must understand the background. We find what we need in Exodus 29:21.

> *And thou shalt take of the blood that is upon the altar, and of the anointing oil, and sprinkle it upon Aaron, and upon his garments, and upon his sons, and upon the garments of his sons with him: and he shall be hallowed, and his garments, and his sons, and his sons' garments with him.*

Notice two things in verse twenty-one. One is the word *"blood,"* and the other is the word *"oil."* Before the priest could offer an offering to the Lord and before the Lord would accept it, the priest had to be sprinkled with the blood and anointed with the oil. He had to be sprinkled with the blood and anointed with the oil before any offering of praise, any offering of prayer, or before anything could be presented to the Lord and be accepted.

147

Before we can go before our Lord, before our gratitude to God can be accepted, before even our praise is accepted, or before any prayer can be made to the Lord, we must also be sprinkled by the blood and anointed with the oil. This means that we must have trusted in the shed blood of Jesus Christ for our soul's salvation. We must recognize that Jesus Christ bled and died for the sins of the whole world. He tasted death for every man. When He went to Calvary, He shed His blood for our sins, not His own.

> *But he was wounded for our transgressions, he was bruised for our iniquities: the chastisement of our peace was upon him; and with his stripes we are healed* (Isaiah 53:5).

When we ask God to forgive our sin, we are acknowledging that we are guilty sinners deserving of hell, deserving to be separated from God forever. We trust in the finished work of Christ through His shed blood for our soul's salvation. As the songwriter so aptly put it, "I must needs go home by the way of the cross. There is no other way but this." Unless you have been sprinkled by the blood, unless you have trusted in the shed blood of Jesus Christ, unless you have trusted Him alone for your soul's salvation, you are not going to heaven.

When we ask God to forgive our sin, trusting in the finished work of Christ for our soul's salvation, not only are we sprinkled by the blood, but we also receive the Lord into our lives in the Person of the Holy Spirit. He comes to live in us forever.

Oil in the Bible is a picture of the Holy Spirit. As I approach the Lord, I do not approach Him on my own merit. I do not approach the Lord because of what I can do or what I have done. I approach Him on the merit of Jesus Christ, what He has accomplished for me through His work on the cross, and how it has been appropriated to me as I put my faith in Him for my soul's salvation. Not only am I covered in His blood but also by His Spirit. He has come to live in me.

The Bible tells us of the holy oil in the book of Exodus.

> *Moreover the* LORD *spake unto Moses, saying, Take thou also unto thee principal spices, of pure myrrh five hundred shekels, and of sweet cinnamon half so much, even two hundred and fifty shekels, and of sweet calamus two hundred and fifty shekels, and of cassia five hundred shekels, after the shekel of the sanctuary, and of oil olive an hin: and thou shalt make it an oil of holy ointment, an ointment compound after the art of the apothecary: it shall be an holy anointing oil. And thou shalt anoint the tabernacle of the congregation therewith, and the ark of the testimony, and the table and all his vessels, and the candlestick and his vessels, and the altar of incense, and the altar of burnt offering with all his vessels, and the laver and his foot. And thou shalt sanctify them, that they may be most holy: whatsoever toucheth them shall be holy. And thou shalt anoint Aaron and his sons, and consecrate them, that they may minister unto me in the priest's office. And thou shalt speak unto the children of Israel, saying, This shall be an holy anointing oil unto me throughout your generations* (Exodus 30:22-31).

In order for the priest to be consecrated to serve the Lord and to approach the Lord and make these offerings, this holy anointing oil was prepared. The tabernacle was anointed with this oil. The vessels of the tabernacle were anointed with this oil. The high priest and his sons were anointed with this holy anointing oil. As one walked in, no doubt, he would smell the sweet fragrances of this oil permeating the air. Surely as he thought of the sweet fragrances of the holy anointing oil, he thought of the presence of the living God in that place.

God has anointed us and given to us His Spirit. Because God has washed us clean by His precious blood, there should be a sweet fragrance given from our lives to a lost world. It should be evident that we have been with the Lord Jesus; we are God's children. We are not of this world; we are of the world to come. We are children of God by faith, and we know the Lord as our personal Savior.

When the psalmist walked through Psalm 23, he said, *"Thou anointest my head with oil."* God has anointed us.

The Bible teaches that when we are saved, the Holy Spirit dwells within us. At the moment we trust Christ as our Savior, He comes to live in us. The Bible describes this relationship in Colossians 1:27 as *"Christ in you."*

We are also placed in Him. By the work of His Spirit, we are baptized into the body of Christ. We become a part of the body of Christ, placed in His body by the marvelous work of the baptism of His Holy Spirit. We are not commanded to be baptized of the Holy Spirit. The baptism of the Holy Spirit is a work of grace that God performs by placing us in His body the moment we are saved. At that same time, we are *"sealed"* to the day of redemption. We receive what the Bible calls the *"earnest"* of the Holy Spirit, meaning that God has given us a foretaste of what is to come.

We are to be filled with the Holy Spirit again and again, dying daily and seeking God's filling, the filling of His Holy Spirit, on a daily basis. When we are saved, God anoints us with His Spirit and enables us to live the Christian life. But, as He gives us special work to do on a daily basis, we should seek God's divine anointing, His special enabling to do the work He wants us to do.

This anointing is not simply for the pastor; it is for every daddy who seeks to be the Christian father God wants him to be. He needs God's divine anointing to be that father. Every Christian mother needs God's divine anointing poured upon her to be the mother God desires her to be.

If you are a Christian employer and you want to be the employer God would have you to be, you need God's divine anointing to have the wisdom you need to lead in your business.

In everything God has for His children to do, in order to bring glory to our Lord, God enables us through His divine anointing. As we serve Him, in a sense, there should be this sweet fragrance or evidence that we have been with the Lord Jesus and that we belong to the Son of God. This sweet fragrance or evidence is the oil of the anointing.

All of God's children have God's Spirit living in them. All of God's children are sprinkled with the blood of Jesus Christ. If you are one of God's children, you are under the blood and indwelt by the Holy Spirit.

The Overflow

The psalmist says, *"Thou anointest my head with oil; my cup runneth over."* Too many of God's children are content to say, "I've been washed in the blood and indwelt by the Holy Spirit," but their cups are not running over. Let us consider not just the oil, but the overflow.

We need to be living in the overflow. Have you ever been blessed from the overflow of someone else's life? As I think of this particular matter, I believe most of us are satisfied with just a taste, and we consider it enough just to say that we are Christians.

We have a Father in heaven who wants to shower us with blessings and gifts. I never shall forget the experience of becoming a father and how I felt in my heart when my wife presented a son to me. My wife and I both knew that God had given us that child. I had in my heart a desire at that moment to do everything I possibly could for that child.

When my grandchildren came along, my wife and I both knew we were in trouble. She said to me, "We are going to be broke the rest of our lives." I said, "That's probably true because every time you see one of those beautiful, frilly dresses, you want to buy it for one of our granddaughters. Every time you see something you think the boys would enjoy, you want to get it for them." We desire to shower them with gifts. We want to do everything we can for them.

Is it too much to think that if earthly fathers want to give gifts to their children, how much more does our heavenly Father want to shower us with blessings so that we can live in the overflow?

> *Too many of God's children are content to say, "I've been washed in the blood and indwelt by the Holy Spirit," but their cups are not running over.*

Yes, He delights that we are His children. Yes, He is joyous that we have been born into His family. We rejoice that we have been covered in the blood of the Lord Jesus and have received His Holy Spirit. We rejoice that we are His children, but that is simply the beginning of it all. Our Lord wants to bless us. He wants to pour out His blessings upon us to anoint us in such a wonderful way that our *"cup runneth over."* May God help us to live in the overflow.

In Psalm 45:7 the Bible says, *"Thou lovest righteousness, and hatest wickedness: therefore God, thy God, hath anointed thee with the oil of gladness above thy fellows."* God has anointed us with *"the oil of gladness."* He wants to make us people who are glad.

Not only does God anoint us with *"the oil of gladness,"* but He anoints us *"above thy fellows."* Can you imagine? Our Father wants His children to have such gladness that they are recognized in this world for their gladness above other fellows. This is not the way many of us are recognized.

Consider Psalm 92. In the closing part of verse ten, the Lord says, *"I shall be anointed with fresh oil."* So many people talk about the Lord Jesus like this: "Yes, I remember when I was a boy, someone pointed me to Christ. I can remember when I asked the Lord to forgive my sin and received Jesus Christ as my Savior. I received the oil of His anointing. The Holy Spirit came to live in me. I was sprinkled by His blood. I trusted in His finished work for my soul's salvation. I can remember that."

But what about the *"fresh oil"*? What has the Lord done for you and with you recently? The Word of God speaks of *"fresh oil,"* a fresh anointing, a fresh enabling, a joyous new beginning. This is not referring to salvation over again. We do not need to be saved again; we have eternal life. The Christian life is not a series of endings, but a series of new beginnings. It is beginning anew. God revives our hearts by the anointing of fresh oil.

What is this cup that overflows? Consider Isaiah 51. We can drink this cup of blessing because our Lord was willing to drink the cup that was bitter. In Isaiah 51:22 the Bible says, *"Thus saith thy Lord the LORD, and thy God that pleadeth the cause of his people, Behold, I have taken out of thine hand the cup of trembling, even the dregs of the cup of my fury; thou shalt no more drink it again."*

God says, "I've taken out of your hand this cup of trembling. I have removed from your hand the dregs of this cup of fury, this cup of wrath, this cup of sorrow, this cup of judgment."

I can live with my cup overflowing because He was willing to drink the cup of bitterness. It is as though Jesus Christ lined up every human being in the human race. It is as though He passed down that line and said to every human being, "I will drink the dregs and the fury and the trembling and the wrath and the separation from God and taste death for every man. I will do that on the cross for you." He did it for you and for me. He took the *bitter cup* so that we could have the *blessed cup*.

Do you not feel in your heart, as I feel in mine, that we have cheated the Lord? We have cheated the Lord because we live such weak, anemic lives by simply talking about our salvation experience. We say, "Yes, I have been sprinkled by the blood. I have been anointed by the Spirit. The Lord has come to live in me. I am one of His children." However, we cannot testify much about our cup overflowing.

The Lord has made a way so that our cup can overflow. Is it overflowing? Do you ever hunger and thirst for the overflow, to be filled with blessing so you can be a blessing? I could call the names of people through the years who have lived in the overflow and have been such a joy to be around and get in on the drippings of their lives. It is a precious thing. If people like that have been a blessing to us, why can we not be people who are a blessing to others?

God has made a way for us to be a blessing to others. I want you to think about this. Many people are not Christians, not because they have not come in contact with a Christian, but because they have not come in contact with an overflowing Christian. The Christian who is not overflowing leaves little to be desired by the unbeliever.

The other day I was speaking to a medical doctor. My question was very simple: "Are you a Christian?" The answer came quickly, "No." In my conversation, demeanor, and behavior, I wanted to create a desire for that person to want to know more about my Christ.

God has all of this for the taking, for us to receive if we desire. Do you ever hunger and thirst to receive it? Can you testify, *"Thou preparest a table before me in the presence of mine enemies: thou anointest my head with oil; my cup runneth over"*?

If I asked the question, "Are you a Christian?" many would say, "Yes." If I asked, "Are you an overflowing Christian?" most would say, "No."

Consider what our Lord said when Peter cut off the ear of the servant of the high priest. The Lord Jesus responded to this incident by saying to Peter in John 18:11, *"Put up thy sword into the sheath: the cup which my Father hath given me, shall I not drink it?"* The Lord Jesus was saying, "Peter, there is more to this than might meet the eye. We are not forcing our way and fighting our way through this. I am going to Calvary to bleed and die for your sins. I am going to pay your sin debt and the sin debt of the whole world upon the cross. I am going to drink that bitter cup so you can have that blessed cup and live the life of overflowing."

Notice what Christ said in John 7:37-38,

> *In the last day, that great day of the feast, Jesus stood and cried, saying, If any man thirst, let him come unto me, and drink. He that believeth on me, as the scripture hath said, out of his belly shall flow rivers of living water.*

The Lord Jesus said, "I am going to do such a work in your life that out of you shall flow rivers of living water."

Our lives resemble more of a little trickle, just barely dripping. We are trying to get a drop or two out of it. But the Lord said, "From within you, I will cause rivers of living water to flow." This is the kind of life He wants us to have.

When He spoke of being the Good Shepherd in John 10, the Bible says in verse ten, *"The thief cometh not, but for to steal, and to kill, and to destroy: I am come that they might have life, and that they might have it more abundantly."*

Many people would like to put a period after the word *"life." "I am come that they might have life."* But the Lord said, *"I am come that they might have life, and that they might have it more abundantly."*

The most dynamic person we meet is an overflowing Christian. This world needs to see overflowing Christians. Lord, make us thirst to be overflowing!

Again in John 15:11, the Bible says, *"These things have I spoken unto you, that my joy might remain in you, and that your joy might be full."*

We sometimes say, "I've been blessed. I have had a little joy in my life." This is not the way the Lord wants it. He said, *"...that your joy might be full."* Sure, in the world you are going to have tribulation. However, the Lord Jesus said in John 16:33, *"But I have overcome the world."*

Are you living in the overflow? May the Spirit of God speak to our hearts as we consider Luke 15. We find here what we call the story of the prodigal son.

> *And when he came to himself, he said, How many hired servants of my father's have bread enough and to spare, and I perish with hunger! I will arise and go to my father, and will say unto him, Father, I have sinned against heaven, and before thee, and am no more worthy to be called thy son: make me as one of thy hired servants. And he arose, and came to his father. But when he was yet a great way off, his father saw him, and had compassion, and ran, and fell on his neck, and kissed him* (Luke 15:17-20).

I love this scene. I can go no further without commenting on the scene of this aged father running to his son. God's desire is to love us, to forgive us, to shower us with kisses, to throw His loving arms around us, and to thrill our souls with His compassion.

The Bible says in verse twenty-one, *"And the son said unto him, Father, I have sinned against heaven, and in thy sight, and am no more worthy to be called thy son."* He would have made a longer speech, but the father would not allow him to make it. Once you are a son, you are always a son. He was going to say, *"Make me as one of thy hired servants,"* but the father stopped him before he could make that part of his speech.

Does it bring joy to your heart to know that once you have come into God's family, you are going to stay in God's family? Look what the father said in verses twenty-two through twenty-four,

> *But the father said to his servants, Bring forth the best robe, and put it on him; and put a ring on his hand, and shoes on his feet: and bring hither the fatted calf, and kill it; and let us eat, and be merry: for this my son was dead, and is alive again; he was lost, and is found. And they began to be merry.*

The father did not give him just any robe; he gave him the best robe. He did not give him just any calf; he gave him the fatted calf. Why? God wants to pour out His blessings upon us.

Some of you are thinking about a bigger house or a nicer car. God may bless you with material things like that, but there is a blessing which the world cannot buy and cannot find. The Spirit of God can bless us with a deep inner peace. God said, "I'm not going to give just any peace; I want to give you a peace which passeth all understanding. I am going to give you the best robe, the fatted calf, and joy unspeakable and full of glory."

It is such a shame that God's children do not live in the overflow. This world needs to see the overflow in our lives. May God help us to live in it, to hunger and thirst for it, and to be able to say with the psalmist, *"Thou anointest my head with oil; my cup runneth over."*

What a Savior we have! When we get to heaven, I do not want to hear Him say, "Why did you not let Me bless you like I wanted to?" Let us receive from God's good hand all He has for us as we live in the overflow of His blessings.

All the
Days of
My Life

"Surely goodness and mercy shall follow me all the days of my life: and I will dwell in the house of the LORD for ever."

Psalm 23:6

God has done a wonderful thing in dividing our lives into days–not decades, months, or weeks–but days. In the creation account, He divided man's existence, as far as time is concerned, into days.

We count our lives by years, but God counts our lives by days. Every day God gives to us is a precious gift and should evoke from us a response of gratitude. We must consider what we are to do for Christ with these days He has given us.

Our lives can become self-centered and consumed with our own interests, but our days are to be given to God. The Lord gave us life; He allowed us to be born. He is the One who provides us with the opportunities we have. We are to yield each day God gives us to the Lord.

The Twenty-third Psalm tells us of the Shepherd's leading of our lives. The Lord does not lead us until we know Him as our personal Shepherd. The first verse says, *"The LORD is my shepherd."* He is not just the Great Shepherd, not just the Good Shepherd, not just the Chief Shepherd, but He is also *my Shepherd.*

Can you truly say, *"The LORD is my shepherd"*? If you can, it is because you have asked the Lord to forgive your sin and by faith you have invited Him to be your personal Savior. Christ told us in Revelation 3:20, *"Behold, I stand at the door, and knock: if any man hear my voice, and open the door, I will come in to him, and will sup with him, and he with me."* You opened the door, and the Lord Jesus came in.

Salvation is not gradual. There may be a sequence of events that leads us to trust Christ, but when we give our lives to Jesus Christ and He comes to live in us, we are saved instantaneously. In a moment, we are regenerated. In that instant when we "faith" the Lord, when we ask Him to forgive our sin and by faith trust Him as our Savior, He comes to live in us.

Being a Christian is more than believing that God is real and that people should be good and read the Bible. Being a Christian is knowing Christ personally. Do you know Him? Can you say with confidence, *"The LORD is my shepherd"?*

The Provision for Our Days

The Bible says in Psalm 23:6, *"Surely goodness and mercy shall follow me all the days of my life: and I will dwell in the house of the LORD for ever."* The Shepherd is leading the sheep, but something is following the sheep–our celestial companions *"goodness and mercy."* God gives us goodness and mercy to follow us all the days of our lives. This is His provision for our days. Goodness and mercy do not follow on occasion but all the days of our lives.

Years ago, I heard a preacher give an illustration about this passage. He had been acquainted with a farmer who had two little beagle dogs. Everywhere the farmer went on his large farm, the two little dogs followed him. All day long, as he walked from place to place, he would turn and see one dog on each heel. So, he named them *Goodness* and *Mercy.* When he would turn and look back, he would see Goodness on one side and Mercy on the other.

Goodness is God's provision of the blessings we *do not* deserve. Think of your family, your health, and the roof over your head. Think of your friends. Think of a child's touch. Think of every precious thing God does for us. God showers upon us His goodness–all these things we do not deserve.

Mercy is God's withholding of the punishment we *do* deserve. We deserve to die and go to hell. We deserve to perish forever. We deserve to be separated from God for eternity, but Jesus Christ took all our punishment on the cross. He showed His marvelous mercy to us.

"Surely goodness and mercy shall follow me all the days of my life."

The Passing of Our Days

The Bible says in Psalm 90:9-15,

> *For all our days are passed away in thy wrath: we spend our years as a tale that is told. The days of our years are threescore years and ten; and if by reason of strength they be fourscore years, yet is their strength labour and sorrow; for it is soon cut off, and we fly away. Who knoweth the power of thine anger? even according to thy fear, so is thy wrath. So teach us to number our days, that we may apply our hearts unto wisdom. Return, O LORD, how long? and let it repent thee concerning thy servants. O satisfy us early with thy mercy; that we may rejoice and be glad all our days. Make us glad according to the days wherein thou hast afflicted us, and the years wherein we have seen evil.*

We find the word *"days"* five times in this passage. Obviously, the Lord wants us to consider our days.

When someone does something for you, you should say "thank you." You may be slow in expressing your gratitude, and you may not even express it properly, but in your heart you are grateful for what has been done for you. Your purpose each day is to recognize God's care of your life.

Think of what God has done for us! He has provided His goodness and mercy for all our days! What are we to do for Him? We say, "Someday soon, I'm going to..." But the Bible says in Proverbs 27:1, *"Boast not thyself of to morrow; for thou knowest not what a day may bring forth."* With no warning, the days of our lives can suddenly come to an end.

The Plan for Our Days

How many great things have gone undone because we planned to do them someday? How many great things could have been done for God? What Christians could we have become if only we had not waited until tomorrow? How many times has the Spirit of God used His Word and His messenger to convict our hearts? We intended to do something about it, but the thought soon left us. The evil fowls of the air, as Christ called them, came and took the seed away. We must act each day upon what we hear and receive from God for that day.

Pray Each Day

We should not live a day without prayer; it is the only way God has designed for us to communicate with Him. It has been a long time since some of us have been in touch with our heavenly Father.

Read Your Bible Each Day

We should not live a day without the Bible. As a pastor, I have the great temptation to treat the Bible as a textbook, a place to get sermons. God did not give the Bible primarily for that purpose. He gave it as food for our souls. We can share with others the overflow of what we get from the Bible.

PRAISE THE LORD EACH DAY

We should not live a day without praise. We can become such negative, ungrateful people. We can see the worst in things, the worst in people, and the worst in the day. We can always find something to complain about.

God has methods He uses to get our attention. He can use pain and sorrow. He can use the life of someone we love. Often the great lessons God must teach us are learned only as things are taken from us, and we are caused to be much more grateful for what we have. But unless we come to the place where we sense with urgency that every day must be given to God, our lives are not going to be what God wants them to be.

We can understand how few days we have to serve the Lord by comparing our days with money earned and spent. Assume you will live to be seventy years old. Imagine that you earn $500 a week. Take the money you earn, $500 a week, $26,000 a year, and change it into $1 bills. Now let each $1 bill represent one day. When you spend those dollars, you become aware of how few days you have to live. Soon $100 is gone, then $1000. Before you know it, $10,000 is gone. In childhood alone, you would spend thousands of dollars.

By the way, we must not forget the preciousness of childhood. If you have children, set your heart on those little boys and girls making their lives count for God. Some of our little boys and girls will not grow up to be adults. The only precious moments you will ever have are when they are small children. Make every day count.

The days pass so swiftly. There comes a time in life when we see that we have spent more of life than we have left. We start giving more consideration to the days we have spent and how foolishly we have spent them. May this bring a sense of urgency to how we spend the remainder of our days. We do not know when we will come to the last day in our lives.

As we grow older, we may face days when we cannot do as we please. We have the idea that as long as we live, we can make our own decisions. But if we live long enough, someone else will decide what we are going to do. In a nursing home we see people being fed because they do not have the strength to feed themselves. They cannot walk where they want to walk; they must be taken everywhere they need to go. Finally, the days of these lives come to an end. Like those thousands of dollars, the days are all spent.

For the believer, when all our earthly days are gone, the unclouded day will begin, that day when we will know no night, no death, no sorrow, no tears, no pain, no dying, and no farewells. But for the man who has never trusted Jesus Christ as Savior, when all his earthly days are gone, he enters *"the blackness of darkness for ever."*

At the conclusion of this psalm, the Spirit of God gave these words to David to pen, *"Surely goodness and mercy shall follow me all the days of my life."* This is so true. Let us desire to make every day count.

For the believer, when all our earthly days are gone, the unclouded day will begin, that day when we will know no night, no death, no sorrow, no tears, no pain, no dying, and no farewells.

As God allows me to live to the end of each day, I want to thank Him. When I lay my head down at night, I want to turn to my wife and say, "If He comes while we are sleeping, we will be together forever in heaven. If one of us departs in the night while we are sleeping, I will see you in the morning on the other side."

If I live to awake to a new day, I do not want to think, "Well, I have another day to go through." I want to think, "Dear God, thank You for this new day. It will be accompanied by Thy goodness and Thy mercy. Help me, Lord, to be grateful for this day, to praise Thee in this day, to know Thy Word in this day, and to talk to Thee in this day. I will never live this day again, and the opportunities of this day will never come my way again. Help me to be grateful in this day and to make the most of it. It will pass and I will never get it back."

Days come and days go until, finally, they are all gone. May God stir our hearts and help us, because of His goodness and mercy, to truly give Him our days.

I Will Dwell
in the
House of the
Lord Forever

"Surely goodness and mercy shall follow me all the days of my life: and I will dwell in the house of the LORD for ever."

Psalm 23:6

---

ll people are headed somewhere for eternity. Our bodies will not endure forever. The Bible calls this earthly body a tabernacle or tent. When we understand that it is not a permanent dwelling, we realize that God has a permanent dwelling place for us.

We do not think of a temporary meeting place as a facility that will last forever. As our bodies are examined, we must realize that they, too, will not last forever. The real person is inside, not on the outside. We are in a tabernacle; we are in a tent. We are in a temporary dwelling. The Bible says, if we are God's children, some day we are going to lay down our robes of flesh and soar beyond the stars to be with the Lord Jesus.

The psalmist said in Psalm 23:6, *"Surely goodness and mercy shall follow me all the days of my life: and I will dwell in the house of the LORD for ever."* These words, *"for ever,"* are powerful. Here everything comes to an end. When someone says, "I'll be with you in a minute," he is simply using a figure of speech; but if you examine the thing closely and give him exactly a minute, you start out with the seconds, and when sixty seconds are concluded, the minute is ended. If he says, "I'll be there in an hour," you give him sixty minutes in an hour, and the hour is concluded. He may say, "It'll take me a day to do it." There are twenty-four hours in a day. When the twenty-four hours are concluded, the day is ended. There are seven days in a week. When the seven days have passed, the week has ended. When the days of the month have come and gone, the month has ended. When the months accumulate to the end of the year, the year is ended.

We mark our lives by days and weeks and months and years. Year adds to year until all the years bring our lives to an end. As Christians, we have with that ending a new beginning that has no ending. The Bible says, *"I will dwell in the house of the LORD for ever."*

We need something to take place in our lives to cause us to consecrate ourselves to Christ. We can then make more of our lives by yielding ourselves to God. What must happen in our lives to bring us to the place where we say, "Lord, I'm willing to do with my life what You want me to do, to be what You want me to be"?

We all need to make sure we have a heavenly home. We not only need a heavenly home, but we also need a good Christian home. Two Christians entering into marriage is no guarantee for establishing a Christian home. We also need a good church home. There is a minimizing of church and church attendance in our day. People need a good church home, not simply a place to go to church.

I have visited John Wesley's chapel in London, England. Wesley was a great revivalist and preacher in England. When considering the lives of men who have been mightily used of God, John Wesley's name comes to mind.

I have a number of books that deal with personalities that God has used and blessed. In most of those books, there may be no more than ten or twelve names on the list. In every one of those books, the name of John Wesley is listed.

John Wesley was born in 1703, and he lived until 1791. He lived a long life. In 1753, he thought he was dying. He was so seriously ill that he wrote his own epitaph for his tombstone. He lived for thirty-eight years after he thought he was dying.

As I think about John Wesley's life and about his serious illness, I do not doubt that God used that incident to stir him. The last thirty-eight years of his life held an intensity that perhaps they would never have held had he not thought he was dying much earlier in life.

What has God allowed in your life to cause you to think about Him? What has God allowed in your family to cause you to think about Him?

When we read Psalm 23, we realize we are passing through this world. We are not going to be here forever. The Bible says, when it comes to the matter of forever, that God's children are going to live *"in the house of the LORD for ever."*

The book of Jude–a book consisting of one small chapter, but a powerful book of twenty-five verses–forms the hallway or vestibule for the Revelation of Jesus Christ. The closing part of verse thirteen says, *"To whom is reserved the blackness of darkness for ever."*

This Bible expression stirs my heart. The Bible says one group is going to dwell *"in the house of the LORD for ever"* and the other *"in the blackness of darkness for ever."* Are you headed toward *"the house of the LORD for ever,"* or are you headed toward *"the blackness of darkness for ever"*? This is a question we must answer. May God pierce our hearts with this penetrating thought.

Entering the Family of God

How do you get into God's family? I have two sons. They are both grown men who are married and have children of their own. My sons came into my family and took *Sexton* as their name by birth.

Some children are adopted into families. As Gentiles, we have been adopted into God's family. Our names have been written down. We are joint heirs with Jesus Christ. We enter God's family the same way we enter our earthly family–by birth. This is not a physical birth, but a supernatural, spiritual birth.

The Bible says in Psalm 23:1, *"The LORD is my shepherd; I shall not want."* Let us look at the first expression of this psalm and the last expression of this psalm. I want you to see the connection. The first expression says, *"The LORD is my shepherd."* The last expression says, *"I will dwell in the house of the LORD for ever."*

Notice the personal references in the first and last expressions, *"The LORD is my shepherd...I will dwell in the house of the LORD for ever."* Notice to whom the verse refers, *"The LORD is my shepherd...I will dwell in the house of the LORD for ever."* The same name is given to God.

When the King James version of the Bible spells the name of our God in all capital letters, *LORD*, this title is from the name *Jehovah* (the covenant God of His people).

> *Are you headed toward "the house of the LORD for ever," or are you headed toward "the blackness of darkness for ever"? This is a question we must answer.*

The psalmist declares that the covenant God of Israel, the God who makes a covenant with His people, is his Shepherd. When I leave this world, I am going to dwell forever in the house of the covenant God of His people. I have entered into God's family.

We do not have to worry about being in God's house forever if we have entered God's family. The matter of dwelling in God's house forever is settled when we enter God's family.

My children are welcome into my home because it is their home. When they became a part of my family, my house became their house. It would not be their house if they were not a part of my family, but because they are part of my family, it is their house.

Because I am a part of God's family, His house is my house. I am a child of God. I have entered into God's family.

I had a physical birth on October 10, 1948. A number of years later as a teenager, I had a spiritual birth when I asked God to forgive my sin and trusted Christ as my Savior. The Lord came to live in me. He became my Shepherd when I entered into God's family.

One day a man took the Bible, turned to John 3:16, and he read, *"For God so loved the world, that he gave his only begotten Son, that whosoever believeth in him should not perish, but have everlasting life."*

He explained to me that Jesus Christ died for my sin, was buried, and rose from the dead. He invited me to pray and ask God to forgive my sin and trust Christ as my Savior. Salvation is more than an emotional experience, though emotion is involved. It is more than an intellectual experience, though there is intellect involved. My emotion, my intellect, and my will were all involved when I took Christ as my Savior, believing that Jesus Christ is God's Son, that He paid my sin debt on the cross, was buried, and rose from the dead. I asked Him to forgive my sin, and by faith He came to live in me. It was not just a mental change. I trusted Christ as my personal Savior. I was born into God's family.

I repeat to you, because I am in God's family, I do not have to worry about whether or not I am going to God's house. Many people are worried about going to God's house, but they need to realize they settled this matter when they were born into God's family. You do not have to fret about going to heaven if you know in your heart that you have trusted Jesus Christ as your Savior. Heaven is your home. You are not going to be *"in the blackness of darkness for ever."* Because you have trusted Jesus Christ as your Savior, you are going to be *"in the house of the LORD for ever."*

I hope you have trusted Him as your Savior. I hope you know that you have entered into God's family. You may be attending a church. You may even be a member of a church. You may be a very religious person. You may be stirred up about something you need and still not be a member of God's family. There is only one way to get into God's family. The Lord Jesus said in John 3:7, *"Marvel not that I said unto thee, Ye must be born again."*

The psalmist could say *"The LORD is my shepherd"* because he had entered into God's family the only way anyone gets in—by asking God to forgive his sin and by faith trusting Christ as Savior.

Enjoying God's Presence

Many people who say they have entered into God's family do not seem to be enjoying God's presence. As a matter of fact, they run after everything else in the world except the Lord. They spend time doing everything except communing with Christ. I am talking about God's children actually knowing their heavenly Father, talking to Him on a daily basis and reading the Book that He has written for us—enjoying God's presence.

As we read Psalm 23, we find this is what the psalm is all about. The shepherd leads the sheep. As he leads, the sheep follow. The sheep enjoy being in the presence of the shepherd. They can see him, and he can see them.

The Bible says in Psalm 23:2-6,

> *He maketh me to lie down in green pastures: he leadeth me beside the still waters. He restoreth my soul: he leadeth me in the paths of righteousness for his name's sake. Yea, though I walk through the valley of the shadow of death, I will fear no evil: for*

175

thou art with me; thy rod and thy staff they comfort me. Thou preparest a table before me in the presence of mine enemies: thou anointest my head with oil; my cup runneth over. Surely goodness and mercy shall follow me all the days of my life: and I will dwell in the house of the LORD for ever.

The sheep gives this testimony, *"Thou art with me."* He says, "You have taken me beside the still waters. You have led me in the right path, the path of righteousness for Your name's sake. You have taken me to the green pastures and through the valley of the shadow of death. I didn't have to be frightened because You were with me." From the lowest valleys to the highest mountaintops, the shepherd leads his sheep. From the break of day to the close of day, from the beginning of life to the end of life, the shepherd leads his sheep.

"Surely goodness and mercy shall follow me all the days of my life." The sheep start out on the journey following the shepherd, grazing, and being provided for by the shepherd. The sheep enjoy the presence of the shepherd just as we enjoy the presence of our God.

Psalm 48:14 says, *"For this God is our God for ever and ever: he will be our guide even unto death."* God does not need to guide us after death because we will be in His presence. We will see Him the moment we leave this world. He is with us to guide us each step of the way even unto death. He goes with us through the experience of death.

Often I illustrate being in God's presence and knowing the Lord by thinking about the sun. The sun covers the earth. We see the light of the sun, and we feel the heat of the sun. The effects of the sun are all over the earth; they are everywhere. There are rays from the sun that we do not see and we do not feel, but they are present with us. The sun affects all the earth with rays of light, rays of heat, and rays that we do not see or feel. The sun also has a location; it has a place.

My friends, God is everywhere. At all times, God is everywhere, not just in our planet but throughout the universe. It is God's universe. But, there is also a place where God Himself is located. The Bible says when we leave here, we are going to go into the presence of God to be where He is.

Eternity in God's House

Let us look at an interesting word that is often overlooked in one of the most familiar chapters in the Bible, John 14. Note this one word that you may never have noticed. The Bible says in verses one through three,

> *Let not your heart be troubled: ye believe in God, believe also in me. In my Father's house are many mansions: if it were not so, I would have told you. I go to prepare a place for you. And if I go and prepare a place for you, I will come again, and receive you unto myself; that where I am, there ye may be also.*

Notice the word *"there"* in verse three. The Lord Jesus said, *"that where I am, there ye may be also."* Do you know where I want to be? I want to be *"there."* I am going to be *there* in the presence of God.

The Lord Jesus said, *"that where I am, there ye may be also."* I am going to meet Him some day. I am going to be with Him some day. I am going to spend eternity with Christ because He is my Shepherd. I have entered into His family. I can enjoy His presence. I pray that many of His children, who act as if they are not enjoying His presence, would confess their sin, get close to God, and enjoy His presence.

Recently a friend and I were walking in the woods over some rocky areas to a beautiful spring. I said to him after we started back up the hill, "I did not even know I had a body until I was about forty years old." Before that, anything I wanted to do, I just jumped in and did it. I did not know I had a back; it never reminded me. I did not know I had sore knees; they never reminded me. I thought I could do anything. Then, God gave me pains and aches just as He gives everyone pains and aches to remind us that we are not here forever.

If we live, we are all going to get old, and we are either going to go through what we call death into *"the blackness of darkness for ever,"* separated from God into eternal hell, or into *"the house of the LORD for ever,"* having trusted the Lord Jesus as Savior.

> *The matter of dwelling in God's house forever is settled when we enter God's family.*

It is not right to say I am one of God's children, that I am going to God's heaven, and then live as if I am going to *"the blackness of darkness for ever."* It does not make sense to say you are going to go to heaven to be with the Lord Jesus forever and care nothing about being with Him here and now.

We have a habit around our house. You probably do something like this around your house also. When my mother-in-law or one of my sons or daughters-in-law comes to visit, we say to them before they leave, "As soon as you get home, call me." We are especially concerned when they have the grandchildren with them, or if it is rainy or late in the evening.

Of course, I could not count the hundreds of times we have waited for the phone to ring, and on occasion we have had to call to make sure they made it home safely.

So many times the phone has rung and we picked up the receiver to hear the simple words, "I'm home." We find comfort, peace, and rest in those words. We are able to put the phone down and go to sleep. "I'm home."

Shortly before I visited my mother for the last time on earth, I spoke with her by phone. She had returned from the doctor and her cancer was worse. The doctor said, "Ruby, there is nothing we can do for you." She had a little talk with my brother, with my two sisters, and with me. She said, "Honey, don't worry about me. God's going to take care of me."

I am going to tell you something, friends. One of these days, it will be a blessed comfort to know we are home. If I die and leave you here, I want you to know something– "I'm home." All is well.

How do I know I am going to my *Father's house?* Because I am my *Father's child.* Since I became a child of my heavenly Father, He has put something in my heart to let me know I am going to His heavenly home. *"I will dwell in the house of the LORD for ever."* I want to see you in heaven. Let us dwell together *"in the house of the LORD for ever."*

The End

Sunday School materials are available for use in conjunction with *The Lord Is My Shepherd*. For a complete listing of available materials from Crown Christian Publications, please call 1-877 AT CROWN, or write to: P.O. Box 159 ♦ Powell, TN 37849

———————————

Visit us on the Web at FaithfortheFamily.com,
"A Website for the Christian Family"

———————————

CROWN
CHRISTIAN
PUBLICATIONS
Royal Reading

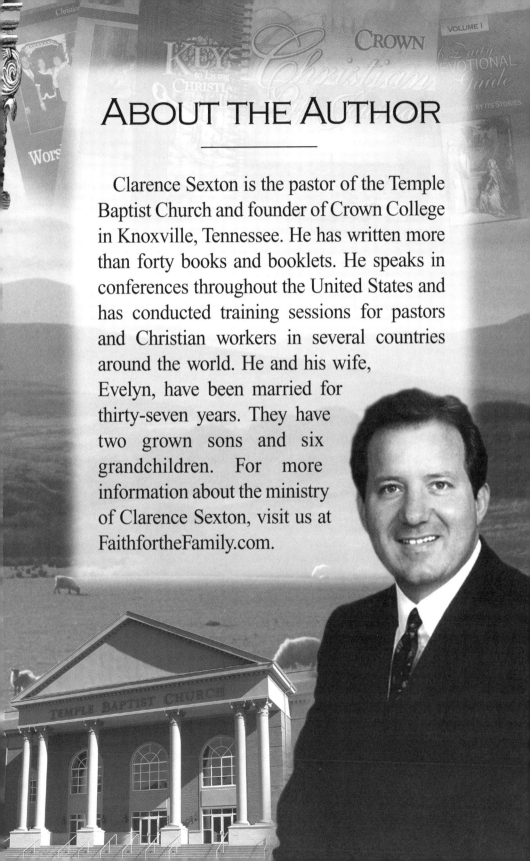

ABOUT THE AUTHOR

Clarence Sexton is the pastor of the Temple Baptist Church and founder of Crown College in Knoxville, Tennessee. He has written more than forty books and booklets. He speaks in conferences throughout the United States and has conducted training sessions for pastors and Christian workers in several countries around the world. He and his wife, Evelyn, have been married for thirty-seven years. They have two grown sons and six grandchildren. For more information about the ministry of Clarence Sexton, visit us at FaithfortheFamily.com.